I0505341

CONTENTS

SELF-LOVE: A SHORT GUIDE TO HAPPINESS AND FULFILLMENT

By Neil Visvanathan

INTRODUCTION

T hank you for purchasing a copy of Self-Love: A Short Guide To Happiness and Fulfillment. I can't express enough how grateful I am to be teaching you the same concepts that drastically changed my life.

This book comes in the form of 20 chapters with each chapter giving a distinct lesson. It covers topics varying from relationships, to self-actualization to improving self-esteem.

This short book should be used as a reference book or a guide book. Feel free to fold pages or highlight where you see fit. If you find a particular lesson that resonates with you, be sure to flip back to it regularly.

Thank you again for picking up a copy of my book. Without further discussion, here's Self-Love: A Short Guide To Happiness and Fulfillment.

CHAPTER 1: WHAT IS SELF-LOVE?

"If everyone demanded peace instead of another television set, then there'd be peace."

- John Lennon

S elf-Love.

What if I told you that Self-Love could drastically change the world?

Big claim, right?

Self-Love is one of the most important ideas in human history. What if I told you that Self-Love was responsible for the Mozarts and Steve Jobs of the world? Would you give me a chance to explain myself or would you write me off then and there? What if I told you that the solution to world poverty is simply Self-Love? You would think I'm crazy! You might even be thinking, "Those kids in the Congo don't need Self-Love, they need food!" What if I told you that Self-Love could solve most problems in your relationships? That doesn't seem as far-fetched a claim and yet all of what I've stated is true, Self-Love truly is the answer to most problems.

Even though Self-Love is the solution to many of our problems, you rarely hear about it on television or in the newspapers. You'll struggle to find a scientific study that quantifies Self-Love. Self-Love is seemingly absent from all popular scientific literature and I'll bet you never had a class about Self-Love anywhere in school, from elementary to university.

Before we go any further, we must understand the meaning of "Self" and the meaning of "Love". "Self" is defined as, "a person's essential being that distinguishes them from others, especially considered as the object of introspection or reflexive action." "Love" is defined as "an intense feeling of deep affection."

Allow me to quickly outline what Self-Love is not. Self-Love is **not** being a narcissist. In fact, someone who is a narcissist is practicing very low levels of Self-Love. Narcissism is bred from not feeling adequate enough which is the opposite of Self-Love. Self-Love is **not** believing that you are better than other people. Putting yourself above others is a very low-conscious form of Self-Love as it only involves yourself in your worldview. Self-Love is **not** being selfish. Being selfish is a side product of being insecure with yourself which is not what we're trying to achieve with Self-Love.

Self-Love means you are fully comfortable and content with yourself. Self-Love means unconditionally Loving yourself. It means Loving that pimple on your forehead that won't go away. It means Loving your friend even though he owes you $80. Self-Love extends from the people you hold closest to the pedestrians you see every day on your way to work. Self-Love does not end with the self (somewhat ironically), it expands from you, to your family and friends and to the greater world around you.

As much as I would Love to keep writing about the intricacies of Self-Love, most people aren't reading this book for the theory behind Self-Love. Most people want clear, tangible ways they can improve their dating life, quit a bad habit, and help create a more peaceful world.

- Relationships. Whether you're in a bad relationship or a good relationship, Self-Love can help you navigate the waters of a committed relationship. Chapter 17 will cover how to use Self-Love to fix a poor relationship and how to use Self-Love to strengthen an already good relationship and take it to the next level.
- Bad Habits. Maybe it's a drug habit or maybe you've got a simple sweet tooth you want to overcome. Chapter 3 will reveal the root cause of your bad habits and the ways you can go about cutting them out of your life.
- Self-Acceptance. Are you fully secure with how you feel? Or do you wish some part of you was different? Chapter 14 will go over techniques you can do yourself to practice self-acceptance until you feel unconditional Love for your body, mind, and soul.
- Self-Actualization. One of the most exciting ideas in personal development. In chapter 7 I will cover the eventual goal of attaining self-actualization and how Self-Love can be a great guiding tool to help yourself find your steps.
- World Peace. Is world peace a pipe dream or is

it really possible? With the right amount of Self-Love, anything is possible. Chapter 20 shows the path of a new tomorrow if we embrace the ideas of Self-Love.

Self-Love has the potential to shape the 21st century in the way we teach, do business and run politics and yet society has hardly grasped it. Why is this?

One of the most self-destructive actions society does is place a stigma on the idea of Self-Love. People who practice the truest forms of Self-Love are either viewed as lazy, or on the other end of the scale, are seen as overachievers. Whenever you encounter someone practicing the highest forms of Self-Love, it slightly annoys you. "Why is this person so optimistic?" you may think to yourself. We see them happy and get slightly angered at the fact they're so content. It's counterintuitive for us to think this way, especially considering mental health illnesses are at an all-time high along with drug addiction rates and suicide rates. Why do we look down upon Self-Love when it has the potential to help so many lives? Some people (especially men) don't like the terminology "Self-Love" as they think it's too girly or Lovey-dovey. It's because of this that they refuse to accept Self-Love even when it could transform their life. The bad news for people who deny Self-Love is that they act in the name of Self-Love every day. Someone may love to hit the gym and think that they're too macho for things like, "Self-Love". That person practices a limited form of Self-Love with their Love of hitting the gym. For someone in a relationship they might only get Self-Love when they're with their significant other. Of course, the goal is to be practicing Self-Love constantly but some Self-Love is better than none.

Self-Love is not a button to be pressed or a switch to

be turned on or off. Self-Love is like a scale that can fluctuate based on who we're with and what we're doing. The eventual goal is to feel so happy with yourself that you feel overwhelming Self-Love no matter who you're with or what you're doing. Self-Love is like a muscle that must be constantly worked on in order to gain its full ability.

Once you realize Self-Love for yourself, you realize that it truly is a magic pill that can guide us to a brighter future. The United States could use Self-Love to remedy the polarization between right and left caused by Donald Trump. Britain could have used a great dose of Self-Love before they decided to leave the European Union. The bankers could have used Self-Love before 2008 to realize how they were setting the economy up for disaster. Far-right and far-left movements in Europe could be handled if people would remember to practice Self-Love.

These changes won't be made overnight. Simply telling someone, "Remember Self-Love!" is not enough to save the political or economic system. Society will have to reach a point where Self-Love becomes a common term to use. Society will have to reach a point where those on top aren't the ones with the most money or fame but those who are able to practice and teach Self-Love better than anyone else. This will not happen in a decade. This will not happen for hundreds of years.

My goal of this book is to make you aware of Self-Love and how you can use it to drastically change your life in the same way it drastically changed mine. The act of you reading this book is the first step into creating a more compassionate future. I hope to give you strategies and tips that you can use in your everyday life to improve your health and wellbeing. I hope to give you insight into the pitfalls in our society and a vision for how it can be. I hope that after reading this book you can find small ways to improve the world around you.

I thank you for deciding to read this book and I promise I will try my best to make it worth your time. Let's start your Self-Love journey.

CHAPTER 2: SPIRAL DYNAMICS

Have you ever tried to get a point through to someone and it never seemed to work? This happens especially whenever politics are brought up. Maybe you have someone at work that you can't seem to click with no matter what you try. What if there was a scale that could measure where your line of thinking was compared to other peoples?

Spiral Dynamics is a model of cognitive development introduced by Clare W. Graves and Don Edward Beck. The model introduces seven levels of cognitive development along with a color label. What Graves and Beck found after thousands of tests is that some people seem to fall into these seven stages. Once you've moved up a stage, it's very hard to regress and move back a stage. Spiral Dynamics is important for Self-Love because the higher you go on the scale, the greater Self-Love you'll be able to feel. Once you're able to pin yourself on the scale, it's easy to find what you need to do to move to the next stage. The goal of this exercise is not to put one stage above another, it's simply what Graves and Beck found from doing thousands of tests on people. You may also find that you don't only fit into one stage specifically. A good exercise is to highlight the sentences you think fit you best. You may find different bits from different stages that give the best picture of who you are. I will give some examples of each stage and it's your goal to identify where you believe you most likely sit on the scale.

Stage Beige

If you are able to read this, you are not at stage beige. Beige is when an organism knows that it's an organism and does what it needs to do to survive. Seriously mentally handicapped people and babies are examples of this stage. Beige is a very basic stage of cognitive development.

Stage Purple

Stage purple is where you start to see humans coming together as tribes. This is how humans would have lived 50,000 years ago before civilization. These tribes would have 50-100 people. You can still find these tribes in places in the Amazon or in remote places in Africa. At purple, the world seems very magical and mysterious as stage purple does not have science or philosophy. Stage purple is about protecting your tribe from environmental threats as well as other tribes.

If you are reading this book you've definitely passed the purple stage.

Stage Red

Stage red is about unadulterated power used to satisfy selfish motives. Stage red rarely cares about what others think or how their actions will affect others. Stage red acts on impulse. Stage red has powerful friends and weapons that it uses to get its way. Examples of stage red would be a dictator or a gangster. Someone who's deeply entrenched in stage red doesn't care how their actions affect others in their mission for more power. Stage red is willing to injure or kill in order to keep a hold on power. Stage red's behavior always ends up backfiring on them, that's why every dictator ends up getting deposed.

Most people reading this will have evolved past stage red.

Stage Blue

Stage blue is where civilization emerges. Stage blue values tradition, rule of law, family, and heritage. Stage blue believes in an absolute Truth and only believes there is one correct ideology. Stage blue typically believes in some sort of God and is willing to sacrifice worldly pleasure for an afterlife. Stage blue believes strongly in morality and believes that someone who goes against their morality deserves punishment. Stage blue is scared of innovation. Stage blue highly values theocracy. Stage blue values etiquette, manners, and dress codes. Stage blue does not like blasphemy. Stage blue is very eager to obey authority and especially believe in divine authority. Stage blue values sobriety and chastity. Stage blue values charity and loyalty and hates traitors. Stage blue values integrity and character. Stage blue believes in hierarchy. Examples of many blue societies are the Middle East, Communist China, and medieval Europe. 40% of the male population of the world is stage blue. Stage blue has 30% of the influence over world affairs. Stage blue finds discomfort with all the other stages. Atheism and skepticism triggers stage blue. Stage blue doesn't like academic elites and postmodernism. Many stage blue people dislike Obama. Stage blue dislikes multiculturalism. Stage blue does not like progressivism. Stage blue does not value disrespect for the status quo. Stage blue does not like sex, drugs, rap music, and rock and roll. Negative manifestations of stage blue are intolerant belief systems, inside box thinkers, and nationalism. Stage blue struggles to have fun during sex. Stage blue prohibits the teaching of sex-ed in schools.

If you find yourself to be stage blue, I will cover how to transcend stage blue into stage orange later in the chapter.

Stage Orange

Stage orange is where capitalism thrives. Most people in North America or Western Europe are heavily at stage orange. Stage orange values self-achievement and "winning the game". With stage orange comes the rise of secularism, business, humanism, popular culture, science (sometimes held as dogma), and the rise of democracy. Stage orange values success and excellence. Stage orange aims to climb its way up the ladder. Stage orange values becoming number one in its field. Stage orange values productivity and optimization. Stage orange is typically great at manipulating resources to get what it wants. Stage orange values results. Stage orange is where pragmatism thrives. Stage orange doesn't typically care about an afterlife. Stage orange wants never-ending growth. Stage orange values capitalism, libertarianism, and entrepreneurship. Stage orange is where self-help starts. Stage orange self-help is about manipulating the marketplace in order to prosper. Stage orange wants to gain as many skills as possible. Stage orange likes charisma, entertainment, and self-reliance. Stage orange values freedom of speech. Stage orange values money, sex, and luxury. Stage orange is obsessed with net worth and tries its best to increase its net worth. Stage orange is consumerism. Brands (especially luxury brands) are very stage orange. Stage orange idolizes celebrities as being the stage orange ideal. Stage orange values sales. Stage orange is all about mass-production. Stage orange believes metaphysics is nonsense. Stage orange is materialist. Stage orange values facts. Stage orange loves data, analytics, models and tries to quantify everything. Stage orange values the scientific method. Stage orange values IQ. Stage orange values creative thinking. A workaholic falls into stage orange. The bottom line is very important to stage orange. Stage orange cares more about competence than your heritage or bloodline. Stage orange values reward and recognition. A stage orange entrepreneur will create products that help people materially instead of emotionally. Stage orange is found in nearly every country in the world (except for maybe North Korea). Stage orange tries to monetize everything. Stage orange is the rise of comedians (who typically make jokes about the rigidity of stage blue). Stage orange leads to the rise of the middle class. The United States is the epitome of stage orange. The movie, "The Wolf of Wall Street" is a perfect example of stage orange. Big pharma, big banks, and big oil are all stage orange. Stage orange has replaced God and holy scriptures with science. Stage orange leads to rampant consumerism. Stage orange leads to corporate lobbying which crumbles democracy. Stage orange views sex as simply "blowing a load" instead of a true genuine connection. Excess stage orange can lead to the mistreatment of animals on factory farms. Stage orange leads to monopolies and deregulation. Excess stage orange leads to the objectification of women which in turn destroys the family unit. Excess stage orange can lead to sex addiction and porn addiction. Excess stage orange can lead to addiction and suicide. Stage orange leads to the rat-race mentality. Stage orange in excess leads to the destruction of wildlife populations and habitats. At the end of it all, stage orange will realize that there was really nothing to all the materialism.

You probably found yourself agreeing with a lot of stage orange. Most people in western societies are stage orange with flares of stage blue or stage green. Later in this chapter I will cover how to grow from stage orange into stage green.

Stage Green

Stage green is introduced when stage orange hits its limit. The transition into green can also be explained as opening the heart and mellowing out orange. Countries like Canada, Sweden, and Germany have all implemented stage green systems. Stage green values Love, intimacy, heart, soul, empathy, kindness, compassion, and mercy. Stage green values liberalism and equality. Stage green is anti-consumerist and anti-greed. Stage green values activism and protests. Stage green people are typically laid-back. Stage green values the flattening of hierarchies. Stage green values other cultures. Stage green values relationships and human bonding. Stage green values pacifism, harmony, and peace. Stage green values intimacy, sensitivity, and femininity. Stage green values spirituality. Stage green is able to be spiritual without being religious. Stage green values the environment. Stage green wants to care about the poor and the crippled. Stage green wants to redistribute resources fairly. People at stage green value intimate sex and care about sexual education. Stage green values creativity, beauty, and art for art's sake. Stage green is willing to express vulnerable emotions. Stage green seeks personal growth to become more compassionate and become more aware of its emotions. Stage green starts to care about new age concepts that stage orange didn't care for. Stage green cares about the soul, spirit, yoga, meditation, energy. Some stage green people are vegans. Stage green cares about talking about feelings. Elon Musk would be an entrepreneur that has one foot in stage green. Stage green cares about nurturing employees. Stage green doesn't like to have flashy jewelry or fast cars. Burning man is stage green. Stage green doesn't like oppression. Stage green is against the status quo, especially if it marginalized people. Stage green gets triggered when religion is used as a justification to oppress people. Stage green is against fascism. Stage green is triggered by corporate greediness. Stage green is against poverty. Public healthcare is stage green.

You might find that although you agreed with a lot of stage orange, you also agree with a lot of stage green. That's perfectly fine, spiral dynamics is a fluid scale and not a rigid framework. You'll find yourself agreeing with some parts of one stage and agreeing with some parts of another stage. Later in this chapter I will explain how to transcend stage green into stage yellow.

Stage Yellow

Stage yellow is rare in our society. Stage yellow is also where the spiral dynamics model takes a leap to tier two. Tier two is becoming aware of the spiral itself and that it has continuous progress. Taking the step into tier two is becoming aware that your view of the world is just a perspective. Stage yellow means not being moralistic.

Stage yellow is careful to not hurt people's emotions. Stage yellow is aware of its carbon footprint. Stage yellow can find a kernel of Truth in what anyone thinks. Stage yellow is radically open-minded. Stage yellow realizes that every stage is fighting with each other. Stage yellow finds ideas more interesting than the community. Stage yellow values systems thinking. Stage yellow values solving the root problem. Stage yellow values taking a multidisciplinary approach. Stage yellow values creativity and thinking outside the box. Stage yellow values ecology. Stage yellow values spiral dynamics. Stage yellow values education, reading, and knowledge. Stage yellow has a dedication to lifelong learning and doesn't let learning stop outside of the classroom. Stage yellow wants to create systems that help all stages. Stage yellow values purpose and vision. Stage yellow values self-actualization.

You've probably found values in stage yellow as well. The more yellow values you have the easier it gets to practice Self-Love. Once you reach stage yellow you realize that there is no end and that you can keep making constant growth and progress to oneself.

Let's talk about progressing stages. Spiral dynamics has an interesting trend where the pendulum swings from individualistic to the collective. Stage beige is individualistic and swings into purple which is for the collective. Purple swings into red which is individualistic which swings into blue which is back to the collective. The further you evolve however, the closer the pendulum gets to an equilibrium. It's also important to remember that you can't skip a stage. If you're stage blue you can't make the leap from blue to yellow, it must be done sequentially.

In order to progress from stage blue you must start to question what you've been taught your whole life. This may be a religion, this may be an authority figure or this may be a family tradition. You must start being more open with the idea of questioning your own views and why you hold them. In stage blue the biggest thing holding you back is the authority you've given to certain people or institutions. In order to evolve you must peel away what you've been taught and start a personal journey to find what Truth really is. Be open to other's perspectives and don't vilify the other stages.

In order to progress from stage orange you must be willing to make sacrifices. If you're really dedicated to overcoming stage orange you may have to work less time at your job. You must start realizing the blatant hollowness of consumerism. In order to progress from stage orange you must overcome the "winner takes all" mentality. You will need to start being against inequality. It will help to find a group of stage green friends that can expose you to new worldviews. You will no longer believe that the invisible hand of the free market will magically solve all problems. Transitioning from stage orange means you start being more open to new-age concepts. You may find yourself becoming less of a materialist. You open yourself up to the ideas of spirituality. You may start doing yoga or meditating. You must stop viewing sex as the act of finishing and instead view it as an intimate connection with your partner. For men, you must embrace femininity as being equal to masculinity. You must become more aware of your emotions and become more secure about expressing them to others.

In order to progress from stage green to stage yellow you must make a drastic shift and start realizing the entire model of spiral dynamics. You must become an avid learner and read as much as you can. A stage yellow person knows that even if they could somehow read a book a day they won't learn even .01% of all knowledge. You must stop vilifying the stages lower than you and instead think of ways you can help others progress up the stages. In order to progress to stage yellow you have to be radically open-minded of other worldviews. In chapter # I will talk about self-actualization which is one of the easiest ways to transcend from stage green into stage yellow. In order to move into stage yellow you must have a clear sense of purpose with your life and strive to make the world a greater place through your actions.

Let me demonstrate how Self-Love is used at each stage and the advantages of advancing the stages. Each stage uses Self-Love in a different way to differing effects. As a person progresses the stages they slowly start to expand their view of Self-Love from themselves, to those in their "in" group and eventually to the world and all organisms.

At stage blue, a person has a limited view of Self-Love towards their nationality, race, religion, or family. Although this person can practice Self-Love towards those in these groups they often struggle to expand their sense of Self-Love to those outside their groups. A person in stage blue typically vilifies other stages and does not show them the same Love they show those in their groups. Stage blue will sometimes feel shame about sex and therefore is unable to fully Love themselves and their partner while engaging in the act. Stage blue struggles to Love other cultures in the same way it Loves its own.

At stage orange, a person's view of Self-Love typically becomes more individualistic and self-focused. A person at this stage is able to respect other cultures and customs although they might still believe theirs is superior.

A person at this stage can Love their family and friends, co-workers, and fellow businesspeople although they may also lie and manipulate them to get what they want. At stage orange a person only seeks sex for the pleasure of finishing and therefore is unable to extend their sense of Self-Love enough to develop a close, intimate connection with a partner. At stage orange Self-Love can be made unhealthy and substituted for narcissism. An example of stage orange's Self-Love can be seen with big pharma, big oil, and Wall Street. Although the owners may have extended their Self-Love to themselves, family and friends, they have not always extended their view of Self-Love to encompass the greater economy, the environment, or the health of their fellow humans.

At stage green, a person's view of Self-Love has been opened much wider and now encompasses nearly all people of all walks of life. A person in stage green Loves anyone regardless of their race, nationality, or family heritage. A person in stage green starts encompassing wildlife into their view of Self-Love and views harm against nature as being just as bad as harm against humans. When it comes to sex, a stage green person includes their partner in their view of Self-Love and wants to be intimate and satisfy their partner. Stage green includes the poor and needy inside its view of Self-Love. Stage green involves all people in its view of Self-Love and therefore feels attacked when a group is oppressed.

At stage yellow, a person's view of Self-Love is so drastic that it includes everyone. A stage yellow person includes people from every stage and therefore wants to build systems that help everyone on the spiral dynamics scale. A stage yellow person includes everyone in their view of Self-Love and therefore has to also Love people we would typically deem evil such as murderers or animal abusers. Stage yellow now encompasses the entire universe in its view of Self-Love and Loves animals and plants in the same way it Loves humans. Stage yellow tries to harbor deep, emotional connections during sex. Stage yellow Loves everyone which means stage yellow must Love the owners of big oil, big pharma, and big banks no matter how much stage yellow may disagree with them.

Now let's dive into how you can use spiral dynamics to improve your everyday life. If you're a teacher you can use spiral dynamics to identify where students are and how you can help them grow to new stages. As a teacher you can use spiral dynamics to create a curriculum for each stage and help students evolve. When building education systems in foreign countries, you must take into account their stages on the spiral. A stage green educator will struggle to teach stage green ideas to stage red thinkers. If you're serious about running a great classroom or a great school, spiral dynamics is essential. If you're a doctor you can use spiral dynamics to help your patients. While a stage orange approach is to simply give a patient a pill, a stage yellow approach would be an interdisciplinary holistic approach and would be focused on finding the root cause, not just treating symptoms. The United States could use spiral dynamics to combat terrorism. Instead of taking a stage orange approach and invading these countries with the military, a stage yellow approach would be to invest in their education, healthcare, and their economies. If you're already interested in personal development and have a successful job, start thinking about whether all the money is really satisfying you. Most likely it isn't. What you really need in your life is more Self-Love which can be found by pursuing further stages of spiral dynamics. If you run a business, start thinking about your business' effect on the economy, the ecology, and the environment.

Spiral dynamics is one of the easiest ways to discover what type of Self-Love you have in your own life. At each stage of the spiral, one's level of Self-Love is different than those around it. I hope after explaining the spiral you were able to find where you sat and are now able to see a way to grow up the spiral. Remember that the higher one goes up the spiral, the more Self-Love they're able to experience. I will be referring back to spiral dynamics in the coming chapters so you may feel the need to read certain sections again to get the proper lesson.

Why Self-Love? Spiral dynamics is essential to see where we're able to progress in our lives. It shows us the beliefs we hold and what's possible for us in the future. We can use spiral dynamics to be more loving and caring people.

CHAPTER 3:
BREAKING BAD
HABITS AND
BUILDING GOOD
HABITS

W e are what we continuously do.

We've all tried to break a bad habit before. If you've ever tried yourself you'll find it extremely hard to break out of the grooves so firmly set inside your brain. Bad habits are created from needing emotional support from something. A bad habit is something you use as a crutch such as alcohol or weed. Let's go over a list of some obvious bad habits and some not so obvious bad habits.

- Alcohol
- Cannabis
- Partying

- Porn
- Video Games
- Television
- Eating
- Biting Nails
- Gossiping
- Being a pessimist
- Being passive-aggressive
- Criticizing
- Overworking
- Getting mad at people
- Other drug addictions

Feel free to add to this list any bad habits that you've discovered in your own life.

How can you tell if you have an addiction? Stop doing something for one week and if cravings arise you have an addiction. You'll find from this definition that you probably have more addictions than you ever could have imagined. Most people believe addictions can only come in the form of drug addiction or porn addiction but really addiction can come in various ways. Maybe you're addicted to entertainment from Netflix. Maybe you're addicted to your work. You might be addicted to overeating. Addictions come from a lack of Self-Love and are responsible for most bad habits in your life.

The first step in getting rid of any bad habit is to take full responsibility. If you continue to be a victim you will only fall deeper into the tracks of your bad habits. Full responsibility must be taken in order to overcome a bad habit. You must also believe that you're capable of overcoming a bad habit. Some people will complain a lot about a bad habit but will never do anything about it. With that kind of mindset your potential is so underutilized and you're not living up to your full potential. You also must try again and again. If you've tried to quit smoking seven times, try again on the eighth time. This bad habit is limiting your ability to experience Self-Love and because of that you must keep picking away at it until you've finally overcome it.

Once you're working on getting rid of a bad habit, you must focus on replacing it or balancing it out with a good habit. People sometimes go wrong with this and simply try to cut out a bad habit without replacing it with anything. You must find a way to occupy the new free time that will open up once you've ditched an old bad habit. Whatever you use to fill your time must drive you and inspire you or else you won't be able to keep up the good habit. If you don't have any strong goals in your life of course your life will be littered with bad habits. You attract what you focus on which means you need to focus on the positives in your life. Most driven people don't have time for television or video games because they're too ambitious and have too many things they want to achieve with their time.

You must be fully committed to overcoming a habit. The first 30 days will be the hardest part of overcoming a habit. It's during these days that your brain will be working overtime to create new pathways overtop of the old pathways that were already in place. Everything will take a little more willpower than usual and it will seem so seductive to fall back into your old line of thinking. If you're not fully committed your mind will think of excuses or will say, "It's okay if I just do it once". It's important to visualize what your life can be like without the bad habit. Think about how you'll feel in a month if you haven't dropped the habit. Think about how disappointed with yourself you'll be and the guilt you'll feel. Imagine what would happen if the bad habit continued for an entire year and the amount of agony and stress it would cause. Think about five years into the future and then think ten years into the future. How would it affect your family and friends? How would it affect your health? Now imagine if you replaced your negative habit with a positive habit. Imagine your life one week into the future. Imagine your life one month into the future. Now imagine one year, five years, and ten years into the future. How proud of yourself would you be? How much more successful would you be? Once you have these images it's your job to follow through. You can't take the first steps unless you know where you're stepping and these one, five, and ten-year visualizations give you the proper steps you need looking forward.

Bad habits make it harder to experience Self-Love because you're not the person you want to be. Self-Love can only happen when you feel fully comfortable and content with yourself and bad habits are like a wrench in the machine. We rarely feel proud about our bad habits and therefore try to cover them up instead of getting to the root issues. My hope is that I've given you insight into how to uncover bad habits and how to neutralize them once you've uncovered them. The only way to experience true Self-Love is to overcome addictions and bad habits to become the person you've always wanted to be.

Why Self-Love? Everything we do is built around the habits we form. If we can build habits that enforce Self-Love we can Love ourselves and the world around us more.

CHAPTER 4:
LIFESTYLE
MINIMALISM

Your life is too fast. Your life is too cluttered. Your life needs to slow down.

The minimalism movement was started in New York in the 1960s and was characterized by extreme simplicity in form, color, and style. Minimalist artists strive to make their art as bold as possible and do this with sharp edges and large surfaces. Minimalism was a way to explore an art form by tearing away pieces until only the essentials were left. Minimalism has huge impacts on art even today with the movement to make living spaces less cluttered and more open.

This is what I like to call material minimalism. What I would like to introduce you to is lifestyle minimalism.

If you're serious about personal development work, haven't you found it difficult to try and grow as a person in today's world? It's hard to stay fit when eating a bag of chips is so much easier than going to the gym. It's almost as though society wants to keep you from improving so it can keep pedaling you food and entertainment. Today's world is not conducive to personal development work. Today's society is built to maximize profit, not to guard the health of its citizens. Don't believe me? Walk into a grocery store and look at all the chips, soda, and candy. These aren't healthy to be eating, but we allow their sale because of the profit they create.

It wasn't always like this. The Romans had a cultural ideal of living the Spartan lifestyle. While today's society is about comfort and lavishness, the Romans (aside from the aristocrats) wanted to live the philosopher lifestyle. While we pamper ourselves in our society today, the Romans had an idea of a somewhat frugal lifestyle, living below your means. The advantages of this lifestyle is it declutters your schedule and gives you time to think. The problem with society today is we spend too much time doing and not enough time being. We're constantly going from one task to another and whenever we get some free time, we're quick to fill it with another task.

I'm not claiming you have to become a monk but there's a lot in your schedule you can probably clear out. If there doesn't seem to be anything you can clear out, then there's your problem right there: your schedule is too packed. You should be able to cut out 20-30% of your schedule. Once you've done that, you need to put 20-30% more time into what's already in your schedule. Whatever is still leftover in your schedule needs to be done with more mindfulness. If you normally scarf down a meal in ten minutes, you need to spend fifteen minutes eating a meal. During those fifteen minutes you need to be mindful of what you're doing.

The highest levels of fulfillment do not come from success. The highest levels of fulfillment come from free time to contemplate and be aware. We believe that we need a busy schedule to feel fulfilled but really think for a second, have you felt the most fulfilled when you were the most busy? If you've ever been on a nature walk through a national park you'll understand exactly what I'm talking about here. Nothing compares to taking in the scenery and the absolute beauty of the wilderness. It's here that you feel closest to your roots and feel more alive than ever. This is the sensation you need more of in your life that your busy life is preventing you from experiencing.

Let's do a quick visualization exercise. Sit with your back straight and your eyes closed. Take a couple of breaths to relax. Be fully present in the current moment. Imagine what your life would look and feel like if you slowed your life down by 50%. Take time to imagine what this would mean with family, friends, and coworkers. Make sure you really think about how you would feel. Think about how it would affect the quality of your life. Think about how it would affect your mood. Really think about how slowing down by 50% would impact your life. Now, open your eyes. What did you imagine? You should have been able to tap into the peaceful part of you and realize that it would feel pretty good to take it slower than how you're taking it now. Some of you may have visualized negatives and might believe slowing down would harm you. If you think slowing down would be negative, that just shows how addicted you are to the fast-paced lifestyle.

Most of us are addicted to stimulation and success. The only reason we pursue success is for fulfillment but that doesn't mean the two of them are the same. You can chase after success and never find a whiff of fulfillment. This is difficult for most of us to comprehend considering that our popular media parades people who have found massive success, not people who have massive fulfillment. We have a culture of celebrating celebrities for attaining levels of success most of us could only dream of. If you ask them if they're fulfilled they will always say yes. If success really equaled fulfillment and happiness why would we see so many celebrity suicides done out of feeling empty? If success was equal to happiness why would our rates of mental health be at record highs? We have a toxic culture that emphasizes success and doesn't emphasize being.

What are the lessons you need to take from this chapter? The number one lesson is to slow down. Cut out 20-30% of your schedule and take 20-30% longer with whatever is left. Be more mindful whenever you're living through your schedule. Remember that success isn't equal to fulfillment. Allow yourself more time to think and "be". Don't always be doing something.

Why Self-Love? By renouncing your busy schedule you will have more time to focus on the things in life that bring you the most happiness. You will have more time for mindfulness and thoughtfulness practices.

Just take your time. Life is about the journey, not the destination.

CHAPTER 5: STORIES OF TRIUMPH

T he world is absolutely full of stories of Self-Love reaching back to the start of humanity. Humans have always needed to find something that drives them so much they'll be willing to give up anything to attain their goals. Sometimes it's just survival but other times someone wants to achieve something larger than themselves. In this chapter I will be focusing on people who wanted to give back to society in a huge and impactful way. Some of these stories date back to the ancient Greeks with Demosthenes and some of them are as recent as today with Barack Obama and Steve Jobs. All of these people had hardship and struggle but were able to make it through with perseverance and Self-Love.

Why Self-Love? All of these people could have easily given up. For these people to achieve what they achieved took an extreme amount of perseverance and hard work. It would have been much easier for them to stay at home and watch TV. Instead, they found something deep inside of themselves that forced them to push through. They didn't give up even after countless failures and because of all their hard work, humanity was able to experience the fruits of their labor. In order to not give up they had to have enough Self-Love for themselves and those they Love to keep striving and to never give up. These stories should give you inspiration for your own life for the lessons you can take from them.

Case Study 1: Demosthenes

Many claim that Demosthenes was the greatest orator in all of ancient Athens, and some believe he was the greatest orator of all time. There was little evidence to prove this at his birth however as he was born sickly and frail. Add to this the fact he had a quite extreme speech impediment. When he was only seven years old his father died and the large inheritance left to him was stolen by the guardians meant to protect him. His guardians would refuse to pay tutors, therefore leaving him unable to gain the education his inheritance was supposed to cover. At a young age he was left fatherless, weak, and unable to gain the education he was entitled to. Demosthenes did not get what he deserved, he did not get what was right. Most of us in his situation would have quit, but Demosthenes did not. Demosthenes once saw an orator giving a public speech. Demosthenes was entranced by how the man could hold an audience with his every word. It blew his mind that the speaker could talk for hours and subdue opposition simply by the power of his voice and his great ideas. Demosthenes realized what he wanted to be and realized he was the opposite. So he took action. Demosthenes would practice giving speeches while doing cross country. He would fill his mouth with rocks and give speeches to practice overcoming his speech impediment. He gained the ability to give entire speeches in one breath. He would stand in the wake and give speeches into the wind to practice his clarity.

Just like today, ancient Athens had a court system. Unlike today, however, you had to represent yourself. After years and years of training Demosthenes was finally ready to take his guardians to court and win back what was wrongfully taken from him. He delivered countless points over numerous speeches until he finally won. Most of the money had been gambled away but this did not matter to Demosthenes, what he had gained was something much greater. Demosthenes now had a reputation as a great orator with an unparalleled ability to control a crowd. This was worth more than whatever was left of a once-large fortune. An academic once asked Demosthenes what the most important aspects of speechmaking were. Demosthenes responded, "Action, action action!"

All of us in some way were dealt a bad hand. There are always people above us who started with more. What we need to realize is that we can overcome these bad hands to create a better situation for ourselves. Demosthenes may have lost out on a large inheritance but in doing so was able to create a much brighter future for himself. It's easy for us to focus on how we've been wronged but we must realize that we always have the opportunity to work harder and stronger than those around us.

Why Self-Love? Demosthenes could have easily given up. He was wronged by his guardians and was given a bad hand. He could have easily thrown up his arms and gone on being a victim. But as he said later in his life, "Action, action, action!" He took massive action in his life and turned it around. This change had to come from a deep part of himself. He Loved himself too much to keep allowing others to step over him as they took what was rightfully his. He Loved himself too much to keep allowing his speech impediment to get in the way of his dream. Demosthenes is the story of a man who Loved himself too much to let the world get him down as he knew he had so much to offer to humanity. He is now known as one of the greatest orators of all time.

Case Study 2: Steve Jobs

When Steve's biological mother gave birth to Steve Jobs she already knew she was going to give him up for adoption. She had originally found a couple that was well-educated, catholic, and wealthy but the couple later changed their mind. When Jobs was placed with Paul and Clara Jobs, Steve's biological mother refused to sign the papers. She only decided to sign after the family agreed they would pay for the boy's education. Jobs was a difficult child to raise and when he was two, Clara and Paul almost thought they had made a mistake adopting Steve.

When the family moved to Mountain View, California, Steve's dad built him a workbench to pass on his love of mechanics. Steve was always impressed by his father's craftsmanship. When Steve was ten, he had become deeply interested in electronics and befriended some of the engineers in his neighborhood. Steve had difficulty making friends with children his own age and was viewed as a "loner." The young Jobs struggled in the traditional classroom. He would constantly misbehave and resist authority figures. Jobs skipped fifth grade and was usually bullied in school. When Jobs was thirteen he was given a Summer job at Hewlett-Packard after he cold-called to ask for parts for an electronics project. In high school Jobs would meet Steve Wozniak, Apple's first employee. In university, Wozniak created a "blue box" that allowed for free long-distance calls. Jobs and Wozniak would split the sales of these blue boxes to make money. In a future interview, Jobs claimed that without a blue box there would have been no Apple.

Jobs enrolled at Reed College in 1972 but dropped out without his parent's knowledge after claiming he didn't want to keep spending his parent's money on an education that seemed "meaningless." Jobs did continue to attend some of the classes and one of these was a calligraphy class. Jobs later stated that if he had never taken that class, Mac would never have had multiple typefaces or proportionally spaced fonts.

Early in 1974, Jobs returned home and started looking for a job where he was eventually hired at Atari. Atari's co-founder said Jobs was "difficult but valuable". Jobs traveled to India in mid-1974 to visit a spiritual leader in search of spiritual enlightenment. After seven months, Jobs returned with a shaved head and with traditional Indian clothing. He experimented with LSD which he later said was, "one of the two or three most important things [he had] done in [his] life."

Jobs became a practitioner of Zen Buddhism while living in a toolshed in his parent's backyard that he had converted into a bedroom. He continued with regular meditation retreats and even considered taking up monastic residence in Japan. His life-long appreciation for Zen is shown in all Apple products today.

In mid-1975, Jobs returned to Atari. Jobs was assigned to create a circuit board for the game Breakout. Atari said it would give $100 for every TTL chip Jobs could remove. Jobs did not have expertise with circuits so he brought it to Wozniak who was able to remove an astounding number of chips. Jobs told Wozniak they only paid out

$700 (not the $5000 they actually paid out) and gave Wozniak $350. After finding out about this a decade later, Wozniak said he would've let Jobs keep the money if he knew he needed it that bad.

In March 1976, Wozniak finished the basic design of the Apple I. Jobs suggested to Wozniak that they sell the computer. They founded Apple Computer Company and the operation that started in Jobs' bedroom quickly moved into the garage. The name "Apple" was decided after Jobs told Wozniak about the All One Farm commune and its apple orchard. To get the money needed to build the Apple I units, Jobs sold his Volkswagen van and Wozniak sold his scientific calculator. A computer retailer would later buy 50 Apple I units for $500 each. Jobs would later spend time on the phone with investors trying to raise capital. Jobs was eventually able to attain $60,000 in funding for Apple Computer.

After the Apple I, Jobs and Wozniak went to work on the Apple II, which would eventually become Apple's first consumer product. The Apple II would go on to become one of the first massively successful mass-produced microcomputer products in the world.

It was after this that Jobs' girlfriend came to him and said she was pregnant and that Jobs was the father. Jobs' entire life was changed by the news. Jobs attended the birth and worked on a name for the baby who he and girlfriend would later name, "Lisa". It was during this time that Jobs was getting ready to unveil a new computer with a female name. Without his girlfriend's knowledge he would call it, "Local Integrated Software Architecture" but later would say in an interview, "obviously, it was named for my daughter". Jobs would continue to deny claims that he was the father and so a paternity test was established that showed him to be Lisa's father. Jobs would give her $500 a month at a time when he was a millionaire. His wealth would quickly skyrocket to $250 million by the time he was 25 making him one of Forbes youngest richest people.

Apple Computers would then get ready to roll out their next computer, the Macintosh. Although it would have high initial sales it would see a sales decline in the next quarter it was sold. This would force Apple to reorganize and Jobs would eventually have to resign from the company. This would lead Jobs into starting his next venture, NeXT Inc.

After stepping down from Apple in 1985, Jobs would go on to found NeXT Inc. After getting the attention of a billionaire, Jobs was able to find generous funding for the project. The NeXT was shown to the world at an invite-only gala that was seen as Jobs' "comeback event". Using the NeXT computer an English computer scientist would invent the World Wide Web. In 1997, NeXT would be bought out by Apple, returning Jobs back to the company he once stepped down from.

After joining Apple again, Jobs focused on making the company profitable again. This meant cutting out many projects Apple had been pursuing. Much of the NeXT technology was added to Apple products. Most notably with Mac OS X which powered the iMac. The iMac would drive huge sales and would be a driving force for Apple at this time. The company would branch out into portable music with the introduction of the iPod. In 2007, the company would take a step into the cellular phone business with the iPhone.

Jobs has had major health struggles in his life. In 2003, Jobs was diagnosed with cancer. After receiving this diagnosis Jobs refused treatment for nine months. Instead of taking the usual measures, he tried using alternative medicines to fight the disease. He would later regret this decision as the form of pancreatic cancer he had was quite curable. In the years leading up to his death there was wide speculation in the media whether Jobs was healthy or not. While the company always said he was fine, Job's health was deteriorating. Jobs would undergo a liver transplant in 2013 to try and stop the cancer. On August 24, 2011, Steve Jobs would announce his resignation from Apple. He would work until the day before he died six weeks later.

Steve Jobs' story is full of him overcoming adversity from day one. Whether it be the bullies at his schools or his competition in business, he always had to fight to stay on top. Jobs' story also had mistakes. Jobs' girlfriend later said that Jobs had apologized multiple times for his behavior towards her and Lisa. Jobs also made a huge mistake with his health that most likely cost him his life.

Why Self-Love? Jobs had to find a sense of meaning deep enough for him to create the first trillion-dollar in history. Jobs had to have the intuition to realize what was best for him at each time, whether it be dropping out of college or going to India to search for spiritual enlightenment. Jobs' story is a significant story of just what happens when someone has so much Love for themselves and for humanity. Steve Jobs is what happens when someone makes their goal of humanity instead of a quick profit.

Case Study 3 : Barack Obama

Barack Obama's story is filled with firsts. Obama was the first president to be born outside of the contiguous 48 states and the first African-American president. Obama grew up without a father for much of his life, only seeing him one time when he was ten. Growing up he struggled to come to terms with his mixed ethnicity and felt like society viewed him differently than others. He spent four years in Indonesia as a child and because of that was able to speak fluently. Obama's step-father would teach him to be resilient and would give him a hardline view of how the world works. Obama would later return to Hawaii to live with his grandparents. Obama would later say that growing up in Hawaii exposed him to a multitude of worldviews that made him into the person he is today. Obama would later note his use of alcohol, marijuana, and cocaine in his youth in order to cope with his identity and who he was as a person. He was a part of the "Choom Gang" which would spend time together and sometimes smoke marijuana.

Obama would graduate from high school and attend a Los Angeles college on a full scholarship. He would eventually attain a degree in political science specializing in international relations and English literature. Obama would find work in law and would eventually head to Harvard for schooling. Obama would become the first black president of the Harvard Law Review which would garner national attention.

In 1996, Obama was elected to the Illinois senate. He would advocate for welfare reform, increased subsidies for welfare and other healthcare laws. He would pass bipartisan laws calling for the videotaping of homicide interrogations making Illinois the first state to do so. In 2003, Obama spoke out about the Iraq war and would speak to crowds saying it wasn't too late to stop it. Obama ran for senate in 2004 and won in an unprecedented landslide victory. This victory would lead to his fame inside the democratic party. He gave a speech in

July 2004 which would be seen by nine million viewers. Obama would cosponsor the Secure America and Orderly Immigration Act which includes guest worker programs, border enforcement, and legalization. The bill was the first of its kind since the early 2000s. He would introduce the Federal Funding Accountability and Transparency Act of 2006 which requires the full disclosure of all organizations receiving federal funds. He would introduce the Honest Leadership and Open Government Act which took steps in preventing corruption through lobbying.

Obama would announce his presidency in 2007 in front of the historical site where Abraham Lincoln delivered his "House Divided" speech in 1858. In his speech Obama discussed issues such as ending the Iraq war, reforming the healthcare system, and becoming more energy independent. After winning the primary with Hilary Clinton, she would go on to give a speech and endorse him. Obama would deliver his acceptance speech to a crowd of 84,000 people and be viewed by 38 million worldwide. On November 4, Obama won the election and he would become the first African American president in history.

Obama's story is quite spectacular. No one would have guessed that a child born in Hawaii who spent a part of his childhood in Indonesia would be president. Obama's story shows what happens when you decide to push harder and further than most are willing to go. Obama struggled with his identity growing up and it led to him searching for meaning through other means. Obama only met his dad once before his father passed away in a car accident when Obama was only 21. Obama's mother passed away two days before he would be elected to office. Not to mention a huge scandal with his former pastor only months before the election. Sermons about terrorism and the division between whites and blacks were found and taken out of context. This could have derailed Obama's entire campaign that he had built on hope and unity. Instead of letting the controversy die away slowly, he did something unprecedented and took the task head-on. He gave the, "A More Perfect Union" speech which would go on to be one of his most famous speeches.

What can we learn from this controversy? We can learn how to use obstacles in our way to make us better. To use obstacles as a leaping board instead of letting them hold us down. Obama took the massive attention that was on him and used it to bring people together. Obama used what was negative press and was able to turn it into a positive triumph.

Why Self-Love? Obama had to care enough about the world to make him want to become president. Becoming president is a hard task but Obama overcame his life struggles to try and help humanity. Regardless of what you think of his politics, Obama tried to create change through Love, unity, and peace at a time when the United States was divided.

Case Study 4: Mahatma Gandhi

Mahatma Gandhi's story is the story of a true twentieth-century hero. Gandhi was born in India and was born and raised a Hindu. Gandhi trained in law in England at the Inner Temple. When he was unable to start a successful law practice in India he moved to South Africa to represent an Indian merchant. Gandhi would stay in South Africa for 21 years. It was here that Gandhi would raise a family and start his first nonviolent protest for civil rights.

Gandhi's time in South Africa was far from easy however. Wherever he went he was treated poorly because of the color of his skin. He was not allowed to sit in the stage-coach with Europeans and was beaten when he refused to sit on the floor beside the driver. Gandhi was thrown off a train after refusing to leave first-class as he had a ticket. Indians were disallowed from walking on the same foot-paths as the Europeans. Gandhi said it was humiliating and that he was disgusted by how people could find such pleasure in such cruel treatments. While in South Africa he would create a unified Indian community that would protest against the treatment of Indians in the British Empire. One time when Gandhi was getting off a boat, he was attacked by a mob of white settlers. He escaped only because of the wife of the police superintendent. Gandhi would refuse to lay charges on any of the men that attacked him.

By the time he returned to India he had made quite the name for himself and was welcomed back with open arms. In India he organized farmers and peasants in order to protest excessive taxing and discrimination. The Champaran agitations were his first big victory in India. Peasants were being forced to grow Indigofera and sell it at a fixed price. Gandhi was able to use nonviolent protests to bring change to the situation and have it remedied. Gandhi was a supporter of the English empire's use of Indian troops in World War I in return for self-governance but was very disappointed when the empire only made minor reforms. Gandhi announced further plans for civil disobedience. This was countered by the Empire's Rowlatt Act which would allow the British government to treat protestors as criminals and have them arrested without judicial review and without trial. Gandhi would tell the British that if they were to pass the Rowlatt Act, Indians would begin to protest it. The British government did not listen to his messages and passed the law. On March 30, 1919, during a peaceful protest, English law officers opened fire on the un-armed group of protestors. Gandhi would tell Indians to not retaliate with violence but instead retaliate with peace. He told Indians to boycott British goods and burn any British clothing they owned. He would say that the only reason the British could rule in India is because of Indians cooperation and that without that cooperation, British rule would collapse and Indians could self-govern. It was at this time that the government would tell Gandhi not to enter Delhi. He would go against these orders and be promptly arrested. After this news people rioted. This would lead to the Amritsar Massacre where hundreds of Sikh and Hindu civilians would be killed while peacefully protesting. Gandhi didn't believe that Indians would ever be treated as equals under English rule and he set himself fully towards self-governance of India. Gandhi would urge his fellow citizens to boycott the English by boycotting English products, boycotting law courts, resigning from government employment, and giving up all English titles and honors. He would encourage all men and women, poor and rich to weave their own clothes. The non-cooperation movement grew massively in India with millions of Indians joining. Gandhi would be arrested on March 10, 1922, and sentenced to six years imprisonment after he asked for the longest sentence. He would be released after only two years.

Once Gandhi got out of prison, he continued his push for self-governance. He would introduce a resolution to the Indian Congress that would call for dominion status from the English. He said that if the English did not co-operate there would be another wave of non-cooperation. The English did not take the letter seriously and did not follow Gandhi's orders. Gandhi would lead another nonviolent protest, this time against the salt tax. Gandhi sent a letter to the viceroy of India stating that he would defeat British violence with non-violence. Gandhi would take a salt march starting March 12 and ending April 6 where he and 78 volunteers walked 388 kilometers or 241 miles in order to make salt themselves with the intention of breaking salt laws. Over the 25 days Gandhi would speak to large crowds of people who had gathered to see him. On May 5 he was taken prisoner in anticipation of the protest he was preparing. On May 21, the protest at Dharasana salt works took place without Gandhi. Webb Miller, an American journalist wrote this about the event:

"In complete silence the Gandhi men drew up and halted a hundred yards from the stockade. A picked column advanced from the crowd, waded the ditches and approached the barbed wire stockade... at a word of command, scores of native policemen rushed upon the advancing marchers and rained blows on their heads with their steel-shot lathis [long bamboo sticks]. Not one of the marchers even raised an arm to fend off blows. They went down like ninepins. From where I stood I heard the sickening whack of the clubs on unprotected skulls... Those struck down fell sprawling, unconscious or writhing with fractured skulls or broken shoulders."

These events went on for hours until 300 men were beaten, most seriously injured and two being killed. After this, the British would go on to imprison 60,000 Indians.

The British government then decided to negotiate with Gandhi. These talks were a disappointment to Gandhi however as he sought Indian independence while the British wanted to keep India as a sub colony. By the time World War II came around, Gandhi was opposed to any Indians joining the military. He didn't want Indians fighting a war for the British when they didn't have independence for themselves. Gandhi would then give his, "Quit India" speech which was his most definitive revolt against British rule. Hours after Gandhi gave the speech, he and the entire Congress Working Committee were arrested. The Indian public retaliated by burning down government buildings and cutting telegraph wires. Gandhi urged people to completely stop cooperating with the British government but to not kill or injure English people, even if it meant suffering or death. Gandhi would be held in jail for two years but would be eventually released because of his declining health. The British did not want Gandhi to die in prison as they knew it would greatly upset India. As World War II came to an end, the British gave clear signs that they would give power to the hands of Indians. Gandhi would call for the protests to end and 100,000 political prisoners would be released.

It was at this time that some Muslims wanted to separate from India and become a separate country. Gandhi was opposed to this and didn't believe people should be separating themselves on religious lines. People would start to riot and Gandhi would visit the most riot-prone areas in an attempt to make peace. Many feared a civil war in India that Gandhi wouldn't be able to stop. The British would reluctantly grant independence to India but would also carve it into India, East Pakistan and West Pakistan. This decision was never approved or accepted by Gandhi. Gandhi would spend independence day fasting and asking for peace from his fellow countrymen.

On January 30, 1948, Gandhi would be assassinated by a Hindu nationalist while on his way to address a prayer meeting.

Gandhi never thought he would grow up and become a leader in the fight for India's independence. The people around Gandhi would have never suspected he would achieve the things he would eventually set out to achieve. Yet, Gandhi pushed through all expectations and was able to drive change to one of the largest countries in the world.

In all of our lives we have events that take us off our planned course. Maybe you got laid off from a job or had to cancel a vacation. It's important for us to remember that these are all obstacles for us to grow and become better from. We can sit around and complain about our situation or we can stand with ten toes down and take on the world. Gandhi could have easily allowed the British to keep stepping on him his entire career but he wouldn't allow it. Gandhi saw the obstacle and realized he could overcome it with peaceful protests.

Are you overcoming the obstacles in your own life or are you letting them overtake you? Are you seeing obstacles as a way to grow or as a way to keep you down? Most of us slip into the latter category and let obstacles get the best of us. Our goal is to be more like Gandhi and overcome these disadvantages and use them to become greater people.

Why Self-Love? Gandhi had too much respect for himself to allow himself to be treated as secondary to the British. Gandhi not only Loved himself too much but he Loved his fellow Indians so much that he wouldn't allow for their mistreatment anymore. Gandhi started as a simple lawyer but quickly became one of the most famous symbols for civil rights in history all because of the Self-Love he had for himself. Gandhi Loved himself too much to let obstacles get the better of him and you should be the same. Love yourself so much that you refuse to let any obstacle overcome you and always look for a way to use it to your advantage.

Case Study 5: Amelia Earhart

A famous author and pilot, Amelia Earhart grew up in an environment where her interests were frowned upon because of her gender. Ever since she was a young child, Earhart had an interest in adventure. Her and her sister would adventure through the neighborhood and explore the outdoors. Earhart made her first "flight" in 1904 when she made a ramp on the roof of her family's shed. She would ride a sled off of the ramp and end off with a bruised lip and torn dress. When Earhart was ten she got her first glimpse of an aircraft that her dad tried to interest her in. Earhart would receive a homeschooled education until she was 12 when she entered 7th grade. Earhart would be particularly fond of reading growing up.

It soon became obvious to the family that Earhart's father was an alcoholic. In 1914 he would be forced to retire due to his addiction. Earhart's mother took her daughters to Chicago where she would look for a school with the best science program. Earhart would eventually attend Hyde Park High School where she would lead an unhappy semester. Her yearbook quote would read "A.E. - the girl in brown who walks alone." Earhart would keep a notebook full of newspaper articles about successful women in men-dominated fields.

Earhart would visit her sister in Toronto and see the returning soldiers from World War I. She enlisted as a nurse's aid from the Red Cross and would work at the Spadina Military Hospital. Earhart would develop a case of pneumonia during the Spanish flu which would lead to some life-long health consequences.

After recovering, Earhart would attend an airshow held at the Canadian National Exhibition. One of the main attractions was a show put on by a World War I ace. The pilot saw Earhart watching and dove at her, expecting her to scamper. Earhart didn't run however and stood her ground. Earhart said that it was this moment that started her introduction into flying.

On December 28, 1920, Earhart visited an airfield where Frank Hawks (who would later gain fame for being an air racer) took her on a plane ride. Earhart said that the ride would completely change her life and make her dedicated to figuring out how to fly. Earhart would work three jobs until she saved up $1,000 for flying lessons. Earhart arrived at her training and said simply, "I want to fly, will you teach me?" Earhart would purchase a secondhand bright yellow biplane which she nicknamed "The Canary." On May 15, 1923, Earhart became the 16th woman to be issued a pilot's license.

After Charles Lindbergh made the first solo flight across the Atlantic, Amy Guest expressed an interest in being the first woman to fly solo across or be flown across the Atlantic. After deciding it was too perilous for her, she called Earheart who she believed had the right image for the undertaking. Earhart flew across the Atlantic with pilot Wilmer Stultz and co-pilot Louis Gordon. The team left Newfoundland and landed in South Wales on a flight that took 20 hours and 40 minutes.

This flight would give Earhart huge public exposure and make her a global celebrity. Earhart would finance her future flights with money from celebrity endorsements. She would accept a position at *Cosmopolitan* magazine where she would use it as an opportunity to advocate for greater acceptance of aviation. Although Earhart had a reputation from the Atlantic flight, she still wanted to set her own records for aviation. Earhart would become the first woman to fly solo across North America and back in August 1928. Earhart wouldn't stop here however as she would then set out to make a solo transatlantic flight. On the morning of May 20, 1932, Earhart set off from Newfoundland with the goal of landing in Paris. During the flight she would fight against strong winds, icy conditions, and technical malfunctions. After a flight lasting 14 hours and 56 minutes, Earhart would land in a pasture. When a farmhand asked how far she'd flown from, Earhart replied, "from America." Earhart would later become the first aviator to fly solo from Hawaii to California.

In 1936 Earhart would start planning a world flight. Other people had flown around the world before but Earhart's would be monumental as it would be the longest flight. On March 17, 1937, Earhart and her crew flew from California to Hawaii. Due to technical issues, the plane needed servicing in Hawaii. While attempting to take off for the second stretch, the plane had problems during takeoff and needed to be shipped back to California for repairs.

On Earhart's second attempt around the world, she planned on going East. Earhart would fly from California to Florida and announce her plans for a second attempt around the globe. The second attempt would make stops in South America, Africa, India, and Southeast Asia before landing in New Guinea. The next part of the trip would be flying to Howland Island, an island only 2,000 meters long (6,500 feet) and 500 meters wide (1,600 feet). This trip to Howland Island would end up being her last due to multiple technical failures from her airplane and the team on the island. Earhart would be reported as missing and a search effort would happen in order to try and find her.

Earhart's life was a life of firsts. She was the first woman to fly solo across the Atlantic and the first woman to attempt to fly around the world. She was a prominent figure as a woman that pushed through social norms and gender barriers.

Why Self-Love? In Earhart's teens she would keep a notebook reminding her of women who were making big strides in men-dominated fields. Earhart did this as a way to constantly remember why she was doing what she was doing. Why are you doing what you're doing? Are you doing what you do for your family? Are you doing what you're doing for a charity you support? In order for us to make a massive change in the world we must first realize why we're doing what we're doing. We must not get bitter or angered at failure and must always try to find the next way for us to push on. We must always prepare ourselves for harder times, we must always persevere and we must always fight for a greater cause.

Case Study 6: Alexander Hamilton

Alexander Hamilton's story is so monumental and famous that it led to one of the greatest Broadway musicals of all time. Without Alexander Hamilton, the United States of America would have ceased to exist in the way it does today. Hamilton was one of the founding fathers of America and was a strong promoter of the United States constitution. He was also the founder of the United States financial system, the Coast Guard, the New York Post, and the Federalist Party. Hamilton was born out of wedlock in 1753 in Charlestown in the British West Indies. When he was only 12 his mother passed away from yellow fever. Most of the family's items were auctioned off. Luckily for Hamilton, a family friend bought most of the family's books and returned them to Hamilton. Hamilton became a clerk at a company that traded between New England and New York. He was briefly taken in under his cousin until his cousin took his own life. Hamilton was given a home by a local merchant as he apprenticed under a local carpenter. Hamilton was an avid reader and an avid writer in his youth. He would receive individual tutoring by a Jewish headmistress.

In October 1772, Hamilton would arrive in Boston and then set out for New York. Hamilton attended Columbia University in 1773 where his fellow classmates would rave about his ability to speak with clarity.

In 1775 Hamilton and some of his friends joined a volunteer militia group. He would drill with the company before classes and study tactics and military history when he wasn't in classes. He would eventually become elected captain and would lead multiple successful campaigns against the British. Although he loved the battlefield, he would soon receive an offer to be Washington's aide which he couldn't refuse. Here he would handle letters in congress, state governors, and powerful generals. He wanted to return to active combat however and threatened Washington with resignation if his demands weren't met. Washington placed him in charge of three battalions in the battle on Yorktown. Hamilton's knowledge would lead to a decisive victory that would essentially win the war.

After the war, Hamilton would pass the bar in July after only six months of self-directed education. Hamilton would join congress but would find trouble when the government could not pay the soldiers that had just fought in the war. Hamilton would find trouble convincing Congress to place an impost on incoming goods. After struggling with how to pay the army, he finally was able to create parts of the constitution which would enforce a strong federal government and the ability to gain taxes. Hamilton would later attend the Constitutional Convention where the constitution would be written out. Although Hamilton was not fully pleased with the final result, he signed it anyway and urged his fellow delegates to do the same. George Washington would appoint Hamilton as the first United States Secretary of the Treasury. Hamilton would be put in charge of handing the nation's debt. He would be put in charge of the mint and would be the reason the United States used a decimal system instead of an eighth system.

During the 1800 election, Hamilton was able to maneuver his moves well enough to pick the lesser of the two evils out of the two candidates. Jefferson and Burr were the two last candidates and Hamilton was able to use his power to have people choose Jefferson who he believed was the lesser of the two evils. It's because of this that Burr challenged Hamilton to a duel. During this duel Hamilton would be shot in the hip and have considerable damage done to his inner organs.

Hamilton's *Federalist Papers* which he interpreted the constitution are still widely used today in courtrooms and studies. He was the founder of the national bank and was responsible for parts of the constitution. Hamilton was always trying to do better than he did the day before and because of that the United States is now the most powerful country in the world. If it weren't for Alexander Hamilton, the world we know today wouldn't exist, and democracy may have not even existed.

What can we learn from Hamilton's story? Massive perseverance and a wide vision. Hamilton had a vision for the United States that he fought extremely hard to make into a reality. In our lives, we need to do a better job of having a vision for what we want. If we're unclear about what we want out of life we can't expect to get the results we so desperately want. If Hamilton's story teaches us anything it's that you need to be crystal clear about exactly what you want out of life.

Hamilton's story also shows what's possible when you're driven enough. Hamilton was able to accomplish more in a couple of years than most of us are able to accomplish in a lifetime. So what's holding you back from achieving more than what you're doing currently? Are you struggling to get to the gym? Just remember how much Alexander Hamilton was able to accomplish. Are you working on a book and struggling to find the motivation to write? Remember that Hamilton wrote 51 essays about the constitution. If you don't think something is possible, look at what Hamilton accomplished and I bet you'll start to reconsider.

Why Self-Love? Hamilton went through a lot of trouble when he was extremely young. His mother died when he was a youth and his father left him. He moved in with a cousin and that cousin took his own life. Hamilton could have been a victim and given up then and there but he didn't. Hamilton dedicated himself to learning, reading, writing, and education. It's because of this that he was able to have such a large impact on the world today. Hamilton had to go deep inside to find the courage and strength that would impact billions of lives.

CHAPTER 6:
ESCAPING WAGE
SLAVERY

Are you happy with your job? Do you finish work everyday feeling fulfilled? Do you wake up excited to do your job? These are all important questions to ask ourselves as jobs will take up around half of all our waking time. In this chapter I would like to introduce an idea you've probably never heard of before: wage slavery. Wage slavery is defined as, "a person wholly dependent on income from employment, typically employment of an arduous or menial nature." Unfortunately, most people are victims of wage slavery. It's not like this happened by accident either, society is like a big pyramid scheme where money gets funneled from the wage slaves at the bottom to the CEOs and executives on top.

It's important to realize if you're a wage slave because that means you are not given independence over your own life, your life is largely controlled by your employer. Your employer doesn't pay you for keeping up with your health or for being with your children. Your employer will not give you time to travel even though life is short and the world is huge with millions of things to see. Your employer doesn't pay you according to the things that bring you the most fulfillment out of life. Most employers however will pay you for doing largely unconscious work.

When I say unconscious work I mean the worker who works at CocaCola selling poison to children. Unconscious work is a secretary working for Lockheed Martin, not knowing what Lockheed Martin does. Unconscious work is the worker at McDonald's selling junk food to families. If you have one of these jobs you may think it's not your responsibility. "It's hard enough to get a job" you may be thinking. "It's not my responsibility anyway, my CEO is the real one responsible" you think. Absolutely, that's why you're a wage slave.

Physical slavery may be banned in many countries but that doesn't mean that slavery can't exist in other forms. The government has essentially domesticated society (which isn't a bad thing) which has led to the vast majority of society being chained up metaphorically. This domestication has led to an unequal society where wealth and power are everything. Wealth is relative, the only way I can be rich is if there's someone poorer than me.

We're usually told that if we want to become wealthy all we have to do is work hard but this is hardly the case. It doesn't matter how hard a teacher works, they will never be massively wealthy. It doesn't matter how hard a worker at McDonald's works, they will never accumulate massive wealth. The game is rigged and largely benefits those on the top. In fact, it's impossible for everyone to succeed through hard work alone because, in order for there to be wealthy people, some people have to be less fortunate! Many people work long hours into the night but some of them grew up lucky. Whether it be good parenting, highly rated schools, or the opportunity to take part in youth sports.

In order to become wealthy you might decide to climb a corporate ladder but you're still in a big pyramid scheme. You may get a promotion or a bonus but you need to realize the only reason you're able to climb the ladder is because you have people under you. Even if you win the lottery, quit your job and move to the Turks and Caicos, you're still in the pyramid scheme of life. You'll have to depend on electricity and oil and gas. You'll still depend on grocery stores to give you your food. Even if you decide to move to a Zen monastery you're going to find a pyramid! There's a small handful of people who end up on television and radio and a large number of people who watch and listen to them. That's why celebrities make millions when most people don't make nearly as much.

Wage slavery doesn't only appear in low-income jobs though, wage slavery can happen with lawyers, doctors, engineers, programmers, and consultants. If you're working a job where you need to dress a certain way, arrive at a certain time, and report to someone higher than you, you may be a wage slave.

Wealth sometimes also comes in the form of knowledge. People who build syndicates have trade secrets they can share with each other as they attempt to gain more wealth and influence over others.

Now, I don't write all of this to make you feel down or to make you vilify anyone. I simply write all this because I want you to see just how deep this problem goes. This isn't simply a small situation, this is literally how your life will be run if you don't take massive action. The default position in life is to become a wage slave unless you do something special. Once you're past your mid-twenties it becomes much harder to change your situation. How does wage slavery happen? Usually from a lack of planning. It happens when you coast through life without a plan or any goals. Most people fall into wage slavery after wasting their youth.

Also take into account how rare it is for someone to have full financial freedom. There are very few people in society who can claim they are financially independent. In fact, too many people think financial independence seems like a pipe dream.

The good news is that there are two strategies to escaping wage slavery.

1. Create massive value, become ultra-creative, be a hard worker, and have a clear life purpose. Recognize the pyramid and think about what you can do for the people within it.
2. Exploit the pyramid. Take advantage of the pyramid and think about how you can extract value from it.

You can either add value to people's lives or exploit value from people's lives. Obviously, I recommend the former. Exploiting people will leave you unfulfilled and unhappy.

What if you choose the first option? The first step is to stop whining and take full responsibility for everything in your life. You don't have the luxury of complaining or making excuses if your goal is financial freedom. You may have been wasting your time up to this point but that doesn't matter anymore. What matters is what you're going to do looking ahead.

The second step is to figure out **exactly** what you want from life. You need to create a vision for yourself that inspires you and gives you inspiration every day you wake up. You need to have a life purpose that guides you and keeps you pushing through even when the times get rough.

The third step is to make the decision whether you're going to be a follower or a leader. It's much easier to be a sheep than it is a leader but the perks of being a leader far outweigh the hard work it takes. Be willing to take the risk of being a leader and see how it transforms your life.

The fourth step is to become a massive value provider. Give out so much value that people feel bad they're not paying you more. Most people can't provide massive value and that's where you can set yourself apart from the competition. You need to be an outside of the box thinker. You can't depend on a business in a box solution, you have to be creative. Don't be a middle man, do something new. You will be paid according to how much you move society forward. Wave slaves give away their creative potential so it's up to you to utilize your talents to be hugely creative. There are thousands of books on thousands of topics, find one topic and find a way to provide value.

The fifth step is to study entrepreneurship, sales, and marketing. If you want to become financially free you'll need to start some sort of business and it's essential to know these three topics.

It's important to ask the question of whether everyone can escape wage slavery. The answer is no, most people will never come close to escaping wage slavery. Escaping wage slavery takes careful planning and five to ten years of work. Is it worth it however? Definitely.

The next important question to ask is whether escaping wage slavery is right for you. Some people are fine with being wage slaves their entire lives. If you're passionate about life and feel like you're here for a higher purpose you may want to put the time into escaping wage slavery. Read as much as possible as it's hard to change your body but it's easy to change your mind.

If you're serious about escaping wage slavery one of the most powerful gals you can set is to escape wage slavery. Another powerful goal you can set is full financial independence. Set a goal to elevate mankind. If you achieve full financial freedom you'll be able to dive deeply into personal development and self-actualization work. If you're young, this is the best age to start.

Why Self-Love? Many people work jobs that they're not happy with being at. Some people are able to break out of the grind by finding something deep in themselves that forces them to strive for something greater. If you're deeply passionate about life you need to find the Self-Love within yourself that forces you to make a big change. You must Love yourself too much to allow yourself to stay stuck in your situation. You must Love the world so much that you want to impact millions of lives and further humanity. You must Love creating massive value for those around you. Most of all, you must Love having a positive impact on the world.

CHAPTER 7: SELF-ACTUALIZATION

In this chapter I would like to tell you about the inspired life. Self-Actualization is one of the most inspiring topics in self-development and I'm extremely happy I have the opportunity to talk about it. The self-actualized is the inspired life and the passionate life. Someone who is self-actualized wakes up every day excited for what's next.

Before this chapter starts however I would like you to take the time to realize how lucky you are to be studying personal development. Very few people dedicate themselves to self-development work. In fact, many people don't have a clue that self-development even exists! Be thankful you accidentally stumbled upon self-development, I know I am. Think about what your life was like before personal development. My life largely consisted of video games before I discovered the incredible world of self-development. How has your life changed since you discovered personal development?

The reason I ask is because I want you to remember what it was like when you didn't have a vision for a better life. Before you realized you could engineer and live out an excellent life for yourself. You still may not realize you can live an incredible life that you thought was never possible. A life unlike that of your friends and your family. A life where you wake up every day inspired and ready for the future.

Everything is about the vision. If there's one thing that school and society are very bad at it's teaching us to have a strong vision that inspires us. Most family and friends set a poor example and live their lives following exactly what everyone around them is doing. This is only made more difficult by the fact we have more distractions than ever. Television, music, movies and video games are all extremely seductive and if you're not careful you could easily lose hundreds of hours to each.

If you're reading this book you may be familiar with Abraham Mazlow's Hierarchy of Needs. The theory claims that there are five levels of human needs and that the lowest needs must be fulfilled before moving higher on the pyramid. At the lowest level of the pyramid you have basic needs such as food, water, rest, and warmth. At the next level above that you have safety needs such as safety and security. At the next level above that you have belongingness needs such as intimate relationships and friends. At the next level above that you have esteem needs such as prestige and feeling of accomplishment. At the very top of the pyramid you have self-actualization: achieving one's full creative potential. Mazlow also introduced scarcity pleasures versus abundance pleasures. Scarcity pleasures being when you fulfill a base need and abundance pleasures being the bliss you achieve when you live to your full potential.

Recognize that there's a difference between a bad

life, a good life, and an extraordinary life. There's also a difference between an ordinary life and the self-actualized life. You should set your goal to live an extraordinary self-actualized life. The ordinary life is like a feedlot, you aren't even aware that there are cows out in the world living on wide-open green pastures.

Try to remember a time where you last felt a huge rush of creative energy. You may have to look all the way back to your childhood. Imagine how great that felt to have a stream of never-ending energy. Now imagine if every day could be like that. Imagine waking up excited and going to bed with more energy than you had when you woke up.

Work can be your top position in life. Work can be the thing that motivates you every day and inspires you. You can use your work to have a meaningful contribution to the world. It's possible to master your career, wealth, health, fitness, intimate relationships, and self-esteem. This is very difficult in today's world as we live in a toxic culture that makes it difficult.

It all seems like a pipe dream but self-actualization is very possible, many people throughout history have done it and many more will achieve it. Self-actualization is unlike the lottery as if you put in the effort and time and fully commit, self-actualization will eventually happen.

One of the biggest problems in your life is you aim too low, you expect too little from yourself. Does this affect your results? Absolutely. You can only achieve as high as you shoot. Imagine if Steve Jobs just wanted to make $5,000 a month? Do you think he would have built a hugely innovative company like Apple? I can assure you that if he had set his sights lower Apple would not have been the first trillion-dollar company. You need to take your goals and multiply them. Not two times, not five times, but a hundred times. You had a goal to travel to France for two weeks? That's a nice goal, now let's multiply it. Set a goal to do a bike tour throughout Europe. Do you want to publish a book? That's also a good goal, let's multiply it. Set a goal to start a publishing business on Amazon where you publish other's books for them as well. Any goal you have needs to be taken one hundred times larger than it is right now. Does that mean you'll meet every goal? Maybe not, but it's important to not limit yourself in any capacity. I would like to take you through some scenarios to help you expand your mind to what's possible.

- Imagine living a life where you never have to worry about money. Always having the knowledge that you can afford any purchase you have to make.
- Imagine living a life where work is like play. Where the best part of your day is work and the work you do inspires and motivates you.
- Imagine living a life where you have full emotional control over all your emotions.
- Imagine living a life where you have a deep understanding of the world.
- Imagine living a life where you have a successful intimate relationship. Finding a successful relationship is extremely hard. Imagine if you could be the outlier.
- Imagine living a life where you have incredible sex. Sex is interesting because sex can be extremely low-consciousness or sex can be a high consciousness activity. There's so much you can do with sex and so much you can learn but most people don't even scratch the surface.
- Imagine living a life where you have full confidence in yourself.

- Imagine living a life where you have the ability to travel as much as you want without having to worry about money. Imagine seeing the world and living with locals.
- Imagine living a life where you finish work with more energy than when you started.
- Imagine living a life where you're surrounded by rich and rewarding friendships.
- Imagine living a life where you're a leader and a role model.
- Imagine living a life where you're able to be incredibly creative.
- Imagine living a life where you're able to break free of the shackles of wage slavery.
- Imagine living a life where you have the time to stop, contemplate and live in the present moment
- Imagine living a life where you're really able to delve deep into personal development.
- Imagine living a life where when you're laying on your deathbed you have a smile on your face because you know you went all out. Having a smile on your face because you know you have no regrets. Having a smile on your face because you lived the self-actualized life.

The goal is not just to achieve these goals but to live them every single day. Most people will go for ten years and not be close to achieving any of these goals. That's why it's important to get started on the self-actualization journey as soon as possible.

Now I've given you the vision I would like to go over some techniques to help you on your self-actualization journey.

- The first step is to find your life purpose. What really

drives you in life? What are you willing to get out of bed every day and set your sights on? If you don't have a life purpose it's hard to find the motivation to work hard towards the self-actualized life.

- Meditation. Start a daily meditation habit. Even if it's only fifteen minutes, make sure you do it every day.
- Self-Inquiry.
- Contemplation.
- Journalling. One of my personal favorites. I personally keep a journal that I write in every day. You can write down what you did, your goals, your fears, and what's been on your mind. You can write as short as a couple of sentences or you can write for an hour at a time, it's all up to you.
- Learn the theory. Read books about wealth and personal finance, take notes, and study your notes. Life is like a test, and it's the most real test of all time.
- Research the top books, courses, and seminars.
- Attend seminars.
- Purchase and take courses.
- Study ancient spiritual traditions. There is a lot of dogma in ancient traditions however so be careful.
- Seek out masterful teachers.
- End unconscious relationships. If you're friends with people who get drunk every weekend you may need to cut them out. You're going to lose them at some point eventually with the type of work you're doing.
- Making new friends. These new friends should be high consciousness friends that are on the same self-actualized path that you're on.
- Cleaning up your diet.
- Yoga.

- Physical workout at the gym.
- Cleaning up your info intake. Being very careful about the news you watch, the music you listen to, the gossip you hear, the content you watch on television and the social media you consume.
- Overcome hard addictions. This would be any addictions to drugs, junk food, coffee, alcohol, smoking, porn, or video games.
- Overcome soft addictions such as arguing, debating, or criticizing.
- Find healthy forms of relaxation and entertainment.
- Take more time to gain life experience. Traveling is a great way to do this.

The self-actualized path is not the easy path to take, that's why so few take it. In my opinion however, the positives far outweigh the negatives. You may have to work your butt off for five years but even if it takes that long, it's worth it.

Why Self-Love? Self-Love and self-actualization and almost the exact same concept. The more you delve into self-actualization work the more you'll Love yourself and the world around you. If you Love yourself too much to be in the situation you're in you should start doing self-actualization work. Self-actualization work is perfect for someone wanting to Love themselves and the world more.

CHAPTER 8: MEASURING HAPPINESS

"What gets measured gets managed."
- Peter Drucker

Interestingly enough, there's some debate whether Drucker was actually the first one to make this observation. For the purposes of today, he was the one who made this quote filled with essential wisdom.

In today's society we track everything. We track the amount of calories we eat, the amount of revenue we make and we measure our performance. We've become masters of compiling sheets of data and exposing what every single bit of it means. The future we once thought was dystopian has now become our reality.

It's surprising that during this time we've left out a

key metric. In our race to quantify every bit of data it's almost as though we've forgotten to track the most basic human traits there are. Even though we could have millions of lines of data for measuring revenue and performance, we still don't measure happiness.

It seems crazy that we still don't measure happiness. Happiness is what gets us out of bed in the morning, happiness is what makes us excited to be alive and happiness is what gives us purpose in life. Without happiness we would cease to function at full capacity. Happiness is one of the most important traits for humans and yet we don't measure it.

Our lack of measuring happiness may be one of the reasons we have such crippling rates of mental health problems in recent times. Ten percent of people aged 18 to 25 have depression in the United States. This shouldn't come as a surprise however as teens aren't raised being graded on their mental health or the efforts they're taking to stay healthy. We only judge based on outdated tests and grades.

There is a solution however, and it was brought forward by a small country in Asia. I would like to introduce you to Bhutan. Bhutan is an extremely innovative country in South Asia. Bhutan ranks first in economic freedom, ease of doing business, and peace and is the least corrupt country in the region. Its number one export is hydroelectricity and it expects to be a developed nation by 2023. Its national animal is a takin, an animal that looks to be a mix between a sheep, a goat, and an ox. It has a population of around 750,000 and its main practiced religion is Buddhism. There's one more thing that Bhutan introduced however that changed the world and that's GNH or Gross National Happiness.

GNH is the leading philosophy behind the government of Bhutan. Is it used to measure the collective happiness of the people in a country. In 2011 the UN urged members to also follow collective happiness as they saw it as a human right.

There are four pillars of GNH. The first pillar is sustainable and equitable socio-economic development, the second pillar is environmental conservation, the third pillar is the preservation and promotion of culture and the last pillar is good governance. There are also nine domains of GNH which are living standards, psychological well-being, health, community vitality, ecological diversity and resilience, good governance, time use, education and cultural diversity, and resilience.

Although Bhutan has received criticism for unrelated matters, one can not deny that they are on the right path when it comes to measuring the right metrics. Humans are the ones living in countries and therefore should have their base needs measured.

Why Self-Love? We need to Love each other enough that we want each other to be happy. We need to want to support each other and the best way to support each other is to measure where we need to measure. If we want everyone to live themselves we need to start measuring their happiness. Bhutan has set a great example for the world to follow and we must follow if we Love ourselves enough.

CHAPTER 9: MEDITATION

Your mind is like a crazy drunk monkey. If you don't believe me you've obviously never tried meditating before because everyone who has meditated knows what I've said is the truth.

Think about your life. Let's assume your mind is a crazy drunk monkey. If you let a crazy drunk monkey take charge of your life will that be the most fulfilling life? Will you be as productive as you can be? That will be a chaotic and stressful life!

Our goal is to find a peaceful and calm life. One where we're able to make proper decisions and always step with our best foot forward. In order to do this we'll have to take steps against the crazy drunk monkey that controls our mind.

Meditation is defined by sitting down, having your mind go quiet, and living in the present moment. Our thoughts are like clouds moving through the atmosphere and when we meditate we essentially cloud watch and examine thoughts as they go by.

Let's go over the benefits of meditation. The first

benefit of meditation is control over your emotions. Emotions largely run your life and determine how much you're able to contribute to society. Meditation is good for eliminating stress. The peace and tranquility after a busy day puts your body at rest and forces you to take a break. Meditation helps you get unhooked from addictions you may have. True happiness comes from being present and in the moment. Seeking simulation will always have a high and a low but meditation seeks a constant happiness. You want to train your brain to always be content with the present moment. Meditation is also good for building up willpower. The prefrontal cortex starts building new connections as early as a few weeks when people start meditating.

There are hundreds of apps that provide brain games for you to enjoy but meditation is the oldest brain game to exist.

Meditation is good for productivity and brain health. Creativity is something that can be heightened using meditation. The best way to practice mindfulness is to practice meditation. One of the most advanced things you can do with meditation is attaining enlightenment. This is the final stage you can reach for.

There are a lot of meditation techniques, today I want to teach the "Do Nothing" technique. The Do-Nothing technique is extremely simple and doesn't take a lot of work. It's perfect for beginners and veterans alike. Let's go over the steps:

1. Sit with your back straight.
2. Have your eyes open.
3. Breathe for 30 seconds. Inhale through your stomach and exhale.
4. Notice your thoughts in the present moment.
5. Leg go control of your attention and your

thoughts.

And that's it, it's that simple!

With this simple technique you can go from being a meditating rookie to becoming a dedicated daily practitioner. I do recommend you make meditating a daily habit if you want to receive its full benefit.

Why Self-Love? As you meditate more and more and your mind calms down you'll find it easier to Love yourself. You'll be able to take the time every day to stop and remember to Love yourself. Most of all, it will help you live a more peaceful life where you're able to put more focus on the things you Love most whether it's family or a hobby.

CHAPTER 10: AFFIRMATIONS

When you look in the mirror, you're not seeing an objective version of yourself. When you look in the mirror you see the parts about you that you like, the parts about you that you dislike, and the parts about you that you really dislike. It's for this reason that we must do positive affirmations every day to remind us that we are good enough and that we belong and deserve the best. When we look in the mirror we shouldn't be discouraged by what we see, we should be motivated and excited that that's the body we get to live through.

Affirmations are things said to yourself typically every morning or evening that enforce positive thinking and a positive outlook. The more you tell yourself something about yourself the more likely you are to finally believe it.

I would like to walk you through some of my positive affirmations and give you some that you can use yourself.

- I vow to escape wage slavery.
- I vow to ace life.

- I vow to live a fulfilling life.
- I vow to gain the ability to travel.
- I vow to wake up every day inspired.
- I vow to become financially independent.
- I vow to be a conscious creator.
- I vow to be a strong leader.
- I vow to have an incredible relationship.
- I vow to Love my work.
- I vow to offer extreme value.
- I vow to live a self-actualized life.
- I vow to Love life.
- I vow to practice Self-Love every day.
- I am beautiful.
- Life brings me only positive events.
- I am open-minded and willing to learn
- Today is a glorious day.
- I have high self-esteem because I honor my true calling.

Feel free to add your own affirmations!

It may seem bizarre to tell these to yourself but you don't lose anything by doing them. Positive affirmations can't do you any harm. In fact, they may have extremely positive benefits for you. Some studies have shown positive affirmations have the ability to reduce stress.

I recommend you give affirmations a try for yourself. Try it for a month and you'll start to see some massive changes in the way you see the world around you.

Why Self-Love? What better way to remind yourself to Love yourself than to remind yourself every day? With affirmations you make sure to practice Self-Love every morning and every evening.

CHAPTER 11: SMALL DAILY HABITS

Our life is shaped by habits big and small. In this chapter I want to go over some small habits you can integrate into your life that will change the way you see the world and the way you see yourself.

I recommend small habits because they're easy to start and they're easy to accomplish. Going to the gym and losing fifteen pounds is a goal that takes a lot of preparation. You need to go to the gym at least four to five times a week and you need to really examine and be careful with your diet. Another difference between big habits and mini habits is that mini habits can be started **right now.** I want to go over some mini habits you can integrate into your life immediately to change your life.

Self-Love Bracelet

We live busy lives and it's hard to remember Self-Love as we go about our days. Self-Love might not even pop into your mind until you're on the drive home from work. That's why I recommend you keep a Self-Love Bracelet. It can be a fancy piece of jewelry, it can be a $10 bracelet you bought at a corner store or it could even be an elastic band. You want to wear it on your wrist as you go throughout your day. Every time you look at the bracelet you want to remember Self-Love. You might accidentally look at it while you're getting coffee at work and when you do, you'll remember Self-Love. Every morning and night you'll remember Self-Love when you're putting it on or taking it off. This habit is great because you can start this habit right now and you can do it with any bracelet.

Finish with a Cold Shower

We all have heard of people who take cold showers. They claim that taking these cold showers is the best thing you could do and that they highly recommend it. I won't be telling you to take cold showers as even I am not at that level yet. What I do recommend however is finishing with a cold shower. After you've had your normal warm, toasty, comforting shower, turn it as cold as it can go for even just ten seconds. Take in the cold, control your breathing and learn to not jump away at the sensation. After a while of doing this it will become easy and you'll be able to stand resilient in the face of the cold water. The next step is to let the water cover every part of you. Do a full rotation under the cold water, get it in your face, really see how far you can push yourself. I've been doing this for years and it's made me much more resilient and it pushes me out of my comfort zone early in the morning. This is a great mini habit because you can do it the next time you take a shower.

Forgiveness

This one may seem simple but it's always the simple steps that are overlooked. It's so much easier for us to get angry and be unforgiving than it is for us to be reassuring and forgiving. In times of forgiveness, it's important to try and control your emotions as much as possible.

Cloud Gazing

A recent hobby I picked up that's one of my favorites is cloud gazing. When you have free time on a sunny day, take the time to lay back and take it all in. We spend so much time indoors that we forget what it's like to be outside under the sunshine. This can also be done at night with stargazing.

Why Self-Love? It's hard to enforce large habits so we must start small. If we start Loving ourselves in small ways it will soon be possible for us to Love ourselves in our entirety. We must start by creating small positive habits before we can move into loftier goals.

CHAPTER 12: IMPROVE SELF-ESTEEM

It's hard for us to view ourselves positively today as we're fed all sorts of content and advertising saying we're not good enough until we buy a product. Our self-esteem has been stolen from us and is being sold back to us bit by bit. In order to help the world as much as we can, we must overcome low self-esteem and be the best version of ourselves we can be.

What is self-esteem? Self-esteem is a psychological measure to determine someone's overall sense of self-worth or personal value. Self-esteem determines how much someone Loves themselves and appreciates themselves. It's often viewed as a personality trait which means it tends to be stable. Self-esteem can include different beliefs about yourself such as how you view your appearance, your beliefs, your emotions, and your behaviors.

Self-esteem has also been defined by Nathanial Brandon as, "the disposition to experience oneself as competent to cope with the basic challenges of life and as being worthy of happiness."

The first part of self-esteem is self-respect. Do you believe you deserve to be happy? Do you believe you don't have to settle for anything in life? Do you believe you should be treated right in a relationship? If you have low self-respect people will treat you like a doormat and victimize you. If you have high self-esteem you won't allow that kind of behavior. People with high self-respect believe they have a right to be happy.

The second part of self-esteem is self-efficacy. Self-efficacy is the ability to have a vision for yourself and achieve it. Do you believe you have a high self-efficacy or do you believe you have a low self-efficacy? When you have higher levels of self-efficacy you feel that no matter what happens to you, you always have control over your life. At low levels of self-efficacy you feel unmotivated and feel like everything was built to hold you back.

You want to have as high of each as you possibly can. Self-esteem is not external, it is all internal. You should be confident and assertive with yourself as much as possible. If you're low in self-esteem and self-efficacy you will struggle to live a great life so it's important to work on your self-esteem as much as possible.

There are six pillars of self-esteem that I would like to go over. You can rank yourself on each pillar to see where your self-esteem is focused and where your self-esteem is lacking.

Pillar 1: Living a Conscious Life. Are you aware of why you're making the decisions you're making?

Pillar 2: Self-Acceptance. Do you accept yourself for who you are?

Pillar 3: Self Responsibility. Do you take responsibility for all of your life?

Pillar 4: Self-Assertiveness. Do you feel like your purpose is something worth fighting for?

Pillar 5: Living Purposefully. Do you have a greater purpose than yourself?

Pillar 6: Personal Integrity. Do you live up to your own expectations?

Why Self-Love? It's impossible to Love yourself fully if you have a low self-esteem. That's why it's important to work on your self-esteem constantly and consistently. Once you're aligned with your highest purpose it's easier for you to Love yourself and those around you.

CHAPTER 13:
CONTROLLING EMOTIONS

W e all deal with the same external stimulus, the real issue is how we decide to react to it.

Your emotion doesn't create your emotions, you create the emotions relative to the environment. Even when the external environment is against you it's possible to change how you interpret it. Doing this you can gain full emotional mastery. If you're living a life where you're not getting the results you want it's because of the emotional difficulties you're going through. The difficulty isn't the circumstance, it's the emotion and how you feel about a situation.

Every time you're hit with a stimulus, whether it be positive or negative, it goes through a filter, and then an emotion is produced. Most people live their lives unconsciously and are unaware that there is a filter in the first place. If we can program this filter we'll be able to take any event and turn it into a positive emotion. It's important to do this because if you don't take any action on the filter you're leaving every interpretation up to chance.

Thoughts create emotions. When you feel happy it's because of the value you place on a scenario. If you get a raise, the raise doesn't come with any emotions. We are the ones who assign the emotion onto the raise.

After a breakup, you can either take it positively or negatively. Some people will let it positively change their life while some people will go through great suffering. You can take it negatively and decide that you'll never find anyone again. You might give up on dating for months and become depressed. Some people may take a breakup and see it as a way to meet new people and start dating again. People who see the situation positively realize they could meet someone even better than their first relationship. You can either see the situation as an obstacle or as an opportunity.

Some people may say that it's more natural to have negative thoughts in a perceived "negative" situation. It's much better however to be unnatural here than it is to be natural. If the natural response is to become overwhelmed by negative emotions, you should set your goal to be unnatural. If you want massive results, you can't be natural. Your natural response is not optimal. You shouldn't want to play games with your health, your finances, or your relationships. Take full control over every situation and find the positive.

I would advise you to be careful about overlooking this advice. Overlooking this advice means your filter will naturally go to the laziest response it can find and the laziest response typically ends up being the worst one. You only have suffered because of your lazy interpretations.

It all leads back to what you want. Do you want to

keep feeling negative emotions? Don't do anything about your filter and keep letting your lazy subconscious take over. This will start a negative feedback loop that will only lead to suffering. Every time we're faced with external stimuli we're given a choice. The problem is that most people choose the worst path which leads to the most suffering. All of this happens because you're unconscious this is happening. Now you're aware of it and have no excuse.

Why Self-Love? A big part of Self-Love is being able to control our emotions. If you're trying to Love yourself you need to be able to take situations through a filter and convert them into positive scenarios. Emotions don't happen outside of us, it's all an inner game. Once you've mastered the inner game it becomes easy to master all of Self-Love.

CHAPTER 14: SELF-ACCEPTANCE

It's an unfortunate fact that most guys don't like talking about things like body acceptance. Many men who do self-development work want routines that they can actively do without having to do much contemplation. While many men focus on self-achievement they rarely focus on self-acceptance and especially not body acceptance.

The first step is to accept yourself inside and out. You don't finish here and lay down on the couch watching reruns however, now you have to take massive action. Once you accept yourself fully you can tap into your limitless potential. Most people are motivated by inauthentic motivations and it's important for you to find what really motivates you.

I have a visualization exercise for you. Sit in a chair or lay down and be in the present moment. Have your eyes closed throughout the visualization. Take time to relax your body. Take a deep breath and slowly exhale. Relax as you're exhaling. Take another deep breath and relax your body even more on the exhale. Be aware of your breathing and your thoughts. Be aware of your body parts. Bring to mind a strong feeling of Love that you've had somewhere in your life. Isolate that feeling of Love. Give yourself that feeling of Love with no strings attached. Relax your body. Start to Love every part of yourself unconditionally. Remember that you get angry sometimes and give the angry part of you Love. Find a part of you that struggles with money and give it Love. Remember how you've been treated unfairly before in life. Give that part of you Love. Find the part of you that has treated others unfairly and give it Love as well. Find the part of you that's critical of others and give it Love. Find the part of you that's been embarrassed and give it Love. Find the part of you that's afraid and give it Love. You may find it hard to give Love sometimes, just remember to give the resistance Love.

Why Self-Love? The essence of Self-Love is to Love yourself unconditionally and through this exercise you'll find it easier to accept yourself and those around you.

CHAPTER 15: 15-HOUR WORKWEEK

American scientists did a survey on employees to find out whether they would rather have an extra two weeks vacation or an extra two weeks pay. Twice as many people wanted the vacation time. When British researchers conducted the study, they asked if someone would rather win the lottery, or work less. Twice as many chose to work less.

John Maynard Keynes is known as one of the greatest economic thinkers of the twentieth century. In 1930, just years after the Great Depression had started to set in he gave an interesting lecture. Keynes would make an announcement that almost seemed to be from another planet. He announced that by 2030 mankind's biggest challenge would be what to do with a plethora of spare time.

It all starts with the Industrial Revolution. An English farmer in the year 1300 had to work 1,500 hours to make a living. In the Industrial Revolution it was common to work twice this amount just to stay alive. Men, women, and children all worked with no days off and no vacations.

Later in the 1850s, some prosperity enjoyed by the top trickled down to those closer to the bottom. By the end of the century some countries were working less than sixty hours a week. A Nobel Prize winner made the prediction in 1900 that workers in the year 2000 would be putting in just two hours of work a week.

Employers were against the idea of a shorter work-week of course. In 1926, thirty-two very important business people were asked about their feelings regarding a shorter workweek. Only two thought the idea had any ground to stand on. The others believed more free time would lead to degeneracy, debts, and higher crime rates. It would be Henry Ford, the creator of the Model-T to introduce a shorter workweek. Henry Ford would become the first to put into place a five-day workweek. Ford realized that if his employees were always working, they would never have the time to buy his cars. He also realized that making his employees work less drove down accidents and drove up productivity. The National Association of Manufacturers which once warned about a shorter work-week was now proudly displaying that the United States had the shortest workweek in the world.

In 1956, Richard Nixon announced that Americans would only have to work four days a week in the "not too distant future." It seemed as though Keynes' prediction was coming true. In the 1960s the Senate reported that by 2000 the workweek would be only fourteen hours with seven weeks off a year.

The problem is that in the 1980s things started to change. Instead of the workweek getting shorter it ended up getting longer. Today, Dutch people have the shortest workweek in the world but are still feeling the effects of our long workweeks. 75% of the Dutch workforce feels overburdened, 25% typically work overtime and 12.5% are suffering the symptoms of burnout. Our biggest challenge is not leisure and boredom but stress and uncertainty.

German researchers conducted a study to try and find the "perfect day." They asked working women what would be included in a perfect day. The largest share of time went to intimate relationships being followed by socializing, relaxing, and eating.

The world is currently in the midst of huge changes due to climate change. Some studies show that a "worldwide shift to a shorter workweek could cut the CO2 emitted this century by half."

There are people who are active proponents against a shorter workweek. There we always people who were against the idea of the vote, the idea of the decent wage, and the idea of the forty-hour workweek.

Just remember, no one on their deathbed wishes they spent more time at work or more time watching television.

Why Self-Love? The more time humanity has off from work the more time we can focus on self-actualization. People are more fulfilled the more free time they have and with a fifteen-hour workweek, people will have the time to focus on what really matters.

CHAPTER 16: THE POWER OF VISION

Vision is a lot more powerful than most people think. Most people find no validity in sitting down and thinking about the future. In this chapter I'm going to explain how powerful vision really is and how you can use it to your advantage.

Imagine getting into a car. You enter with a full tank of gas and lots of enthusiasm. You start driving. And then you drive some more. And then you drive some more. You keep driving until you run out of gas or something stops you. Why did you start driving around aimlessly? Because you didn't have a sense of direction, purpose, or a vision of the destination.

I would like to introduce you to the Law of Attraction. The Law of Attraction states that what you focus on is what you tend to get. It can be used both positively or negatively. If you focus on the positives, you'll bring more positive events into your life while if you focus on the negatives you'll bring more negative events into your life.

Most people have no control over this part of their mind and have it slip from positive to negative at a whims notice. By default the mind typically falls into negative patterns. This is because of basic human survival, it's important for us to be aware of survival constantly. The only time this doesn't help us is during modern civilization. We rarely have to worry about neighboring tribes and lion attacks. It's extremely hard for us to achieve anything while our mind is constantly focusing on the negative events.

You need to stop focusing on failure. It's only taking you down a negative feedback loop. You also need to stop focusing on why you can't achieve something. It's only taking you further away from your goals.

You need to envision a hero's journey for yourself. The hero's journey is a literary device used to show the change someone makes over the course of a story. Your life needs to be a hero's journey. At the start you may turn away when your life purpose calls upon you. You may even turn away a couple of times. At some point you decide to make a difference though and you escape from your old life. You head out onto the path less traveled in search of the holy grail. The holy grail is a metaphor for your life purpose. On your journey you meet many deadly monsters but you fight through them one by one. Sometimes you meet a monster so huge that you're scared at first. You may lose the fight the first couple of times but eventually you win. And finally after years or even decades of fighting you reach the holy grail. You return a changed person and you return ready to give your knowledge to anyone who's eager to hear your story.

Start to only focus on the things you want to create. If you want a great job, start to focus on what a great job would look like. If you want a great relationship, focus on what a great relationship would look like. Carefully train yourself to focus on your vision every day.

A great example of this is the pyramids. The pyramids would have taken decades to complete and would have been extremely difficult to oversee. The visionary behind the pyramids would have had to hold the vision for two or three decades before the pyramids came into fruition. Imagine if the pyramids wouldn't have been built because of their cost. Imagine if the pyramids wouldn't have been built because the labor was too difficult to figure out. Imagine if the pyramids weren't built because of the politics at the time. The people overseeing the pyramids had a more noble vision of what was possible and were willing to make it work.

Why Self-Love? In order to Love yourself you need to have a vision for your life that inspires you. You need to wake up every day inspired and motivated and that can't happen unless you have an invigorating vision for your future.

CHAPTER 17: DEALING WITH BAD RELATIONSHIPS

Most people know if they're in a poor relationship right?

Wrong.

There are thousands of people in bad relationships who don't even realize they're in a bad relationship. You've probably seen it for yourself with friends who refuse to break up with their toxic boyfriend or girlfriend. You don't understand how they could stay in a bad relationship. Take a step back and realize for a second that it could easily be you in their situation. Most relationships are not healthy relationships, most have huge problems.

There are three kinds of relationships. Codependent relationships, independent relationships, and interdependent relationships. If you keep finding yourself in bad relationships it's most likely because you're in the codependent section. Codependency is where two people in a relationship use the other as emotional crutches in a relationship. The next level is an independent relationship. Both members are strong on their own but they don't synergize very well. The last level is the interdependent relationship. The two of them work together and create a sum greater than the whole of its parts.

Most people don't like to admit that they're in a co-dependent relationship. It sounds like you're enabling the other person. What it really means is that you struggle to be happy and fulfilled on your own.

The reason this happens is because both people in a relationship have flaws that they're not willing to admit to. The problem is found within each of us, not outside of us. This is why it's so tricky because the brain likes to create scenarios where it's the other person's fault. This doesn't mean the other person isn't doing anything wrong but it does mean that you need to take 100% responsibility for your own actions.

You also have to bite the bullet and realize that all your relationship problems won't end the moment you decide to end the relationship. If you have a vision of leaving a bad relationship, finding the right person, and living a happy life together, it will never happen. Unless you're willing to go inside yourself and do the introspective work it's impossible to have a stable relationship.

Going inside is not easy, it's one of the hardest things you can do. If you want to have a positive relationship however, you can't overlook introspection.

You need to look inside and see why you need Love so bad. Why don't you feel good enough by yourself? Were you neglected as a youth and denied Love from your guardians? Have you had bad relationships in the past which ruined your ability to have a positive one today?

Why Self-Love? In order to Love others you must be able to Love yourself first. Once you're able to Love yourself you can Love those around you. If you're in a bad relationship, you're not expressing Self-Love as you're not Loving yourself enough to leave a negative relationship. Self-Love is the most important thing when it comes to having a positive relationship.

CHAPTER 18:
SOCIAL MEDIA
DETOX

A s I write these words I'm in the middle of a detox. This isn't a typical "green smoothie" detox or a carbs detox. I'm in the middle of a social media detox.

I'm taking it a step further however. No social media, no drug use, no video games, "no fap" and no music. I'm planning on continuing the detox for a week. I have to say, it's been one of the hardest weeks of my life.

But also one of the most transformative.

I set three goals for the week. Write at least 500 words a day in this book, finish a life purpose course I'm currently enrolled in and make content for developed-mind.org.

The reason I wanted to do a social media detox and why I recommend it for others is because most of us are addicted. If you can't go a week without something without having strong urges, you're addicted. Most of us can barely go a day without checking our Facebook or Instagram.

In an experiment on rats they had a piece of food and a button that would give the rat a hit of dopamine every time the button was clicked. Once the rat realized the button would release instant pleasure, the rat would forgo everything to keep clicking the button. In fact, the rat was willing to walk across an electrical grid and be shocked in order to keep getting those hits of dopamine. That's what social media is like for our brains. It gives us a consistent hit of dopamine that we can attain anytime we open up a social media application. When we should be sleeping, we're willing to walk across that electrical grid and be shocked for the sake of getting dopamine hits.

If you're reading this, I recommend you try a social media detox. It will be a struggle at first but over time you'll find yourself becoming more productive and having more energy.

Why Self-Love? Self-Love can't happen if you're distracted. In order to practice Self-Love properly you must be able to have full focus on it. Your mind needs to be focused on how you can better yourself, not how to cross the electrical grid.

CHAPTER 19:
UNIVERSAL
BASIC INCOME

We like to pretend that the free market will solve all our problems. The fact of the matter is that this is no longer the case.

Let's start with inequality. The share of GDP going to wages has fallen from 54% in 1970 to 44% in 2013. All this while the share of GDP going to corporate profits has gone from 4% to 11%. In America, the top 1% have collected 52% of the real income growth since 2009.

Americans find themselves with pockets tighter than ever. "A Bankrate survey in 2017 found that 59 percent of Americans don't have the savings to pay an unexpected expense of $500 and would need to put it on a credit card, ask for help or cut back for several months to manage it." A similar survey found that 75% could not pay a $400 payment from their checking or savings account if an emergency arose.

Things aren't looking any better either. Many workers are at risk of losing their jobs to automation. A consulting company makes the claim that between 64% and 69% of data collecting and processing tasks that are commonplace in admin settings are automatable. That same consulting company estimates that 73% of food prep jobs are automatable.

Due to online retailers such as Amazon, traditional retail is closing down. A sobering fact is that "the equivalent of 52 Malls of America are closing in 2017, or once per week." Traditional retail is being pushed out of the picture.

Things aren't any better for factory workers and truck drivers. After 2000, more than five million manufacturing workers lost their jobs, 80% being lost to automation. In 29 states, truck driving is the most common occupation and nearly 7.2 million workers depend on the trucking industry to feed their families. Examples are people working at motels, diners and truck stops.

The finance industry isn't safe either. Most tasks are repetitive and logical making them ripe for automation. "Goldman Sachs went from 600 NYSE traders in 2000 to just two in 2017 supported by 200 computer engineers."

This problem with automation and jobs did not happen randomly however, it's of our doing. A cab driver can cook, raise a family, and love music but when we get into the back of the taxi we just want him or her to be a taxi driver.

Our long term unemployment is becoming a huge problem. Long term unemployment is one of the most destructive things that can happen to a human alongside the death of a loved one or permanent injury. Once the happiness levels tank, they never recover. People who have been unemployed for long stretches of time lose skills and employers see them as a risk.

So what do we do in this age of unprecedented change and innovation? We call for radical but much-needed policy. A universal basic income would be one of those policies. In fact,, article 25 of the Universal Declaration of Human Rights says so.

Giving people free money would never work though right? Wouldn't poor people just use it to spend more money on drugs?

"London, May 2009 - An experiment is underway. Its subjects: thirteen homeless men. They are veterans of the street. Some have been sleeping on the cold pavement of the Square Mile, Europe's financial center, for going on forty years. Between the police expenses, court costs, and social services, these thirteen troublemakers have racked up a bill estimated at £400,000 ($650,000) or more. Per year."

The city finally had enough and decided to run an experiment: what if we gave them money directly? Would they spend it on frivolous things or would they use it to get off the streets? They were given £3,000 in spending money and sent on their way. The program was a huge success with seven out of the thirteen getting a roof over their head. The cost of this program? £50,000 a year.

There are examples of this all over the globe. Bernard Omondi was earning $2 a day as a worker in a stone quarry in Kenya until he was given $500. This was almost a year's salary to him. He used the money to buy a motor-cycle from India which he uses to taxi people around making three times his wage at the quarry.

Researchers at the University of Manchester found four things: "(1) households put the money to good use, (2) poverty declines, (3) there can be diverse long-term benefits for income, health and tax revenues, and (4) the programs cost less than the alternatives." A universal basic income experiment was run in Canada in 1973 in a small town named Dauphin. Everyone in the town was guaranteed a basic income, making sure that no one fell below the poverty line. Economists wanted to see whether people would work less, sociologists would see the effects on family life and researchers placed themselves in the community to see how people would react. The project was shut down after the introduction of a conservative government and the results wouldn't be looked over until many years later. Once they looked at the results, how did the project fare?

The experiment had been a success.

"Young adults postponed getting married, and birth rates dropped. Their school performance improved substantially." Rates of hospitalization went down and working hours hardly went down at all. This isn't to mention all the positive things people did with the money.

"One mother who had dropped out of high school worked less in order to earn a degree in psychology and get a job as a researcher. Another woman took acting classes; her husband began composing music."

The data all points in one direction: giving people money works. The only problem is, how do we make it a reality?

Making Universal Basic Income a Reality

Andrew Yang, the founder of Venture For America and a Democratic presidential candidate proposed a solution. He says that everyone over the age of 18 should be given $1,000 a month or $12,000 a year. In order to pay for this plan, he proposed a VAT (value-added tax) of 10%.

"The hedge fund billionaire who spends $10 million a year on private jets and fancy cars will pay $1 million into the system and receive $12,000. The single mom will pay about $2,500 and receive $12,000, and will also have the peace of mind that her child will start receiving $1,000 a month when he or she graduates from high school.

Most of the money given will be spent by people who need it most and go right back into the communities that need it most.

A universal basic income has been spoken about for centuries by very well known people. Martin Luther King Jr once said: "I am now convinced that the simplest approach will prove to be the most effective-the solution to poverty is to abolish it directly by a now widely discussed measure: the guaranteed income."

Richard Nixon stated: "What I am proposing is that the Federal Government build a foundation under the income of every American family...that cannot care for itself-and wherever in America that family may live."

Bernie Sanders is quoted as saying: "In my view, every American is entitled to at least a minimum standard of living... There are different ways to get to that goal, but that's the goal we should strive to reach."

Stephen Hawking said this: "Everyone can enjoy a life of luxurious leisure if the machine-produced wealth is shared, or more people can end up miserably poor if the machine owners successfully lobby against wealth redistribution. So far, the trend seems to be toward the second option, with technology driving ever-increasing inequality."

Even Barack Obama has had a say on the issue. In 2016 he was quoted saying: "The way I describe it is that, because of automation, because of globalization, we're going to have to examine the social compact, the same way we did early in the 19th century and then again during and after the Great Depression. The notion of a 40-hour workweek, a minimum wage, child labor laws, etc.- those will have to be updated for these new realities." He spoke about the issue again saying: "What is indisputable... is that as AI gets further incorporated, and the society potentially gets wealthier, the link between production and distribution, how much you work and how much you make, gets further and further attenuated... we'll be debating unconditional free money over the next 10 to 20 years."

It's not only an idea shared by politicians, billionaires such as Warren Buffett, Bill Gates, Elon Musk and Mark Zuckerberg have all weighed in favor of a universal basic income.

It only makes sense. "An analysis by the Roosevelt Institute of this $12,000 per year per adult proposal found that adopting it would permanently grow the (United States) economy by 12.56 to 13.10 percent."

Why Self-Love? We have to overcome the idea that everyone gets something for free, whether they've earned it or not. We have to look at the data and realize that a universal basic income would benefit all of us. We have to stop being selfish and take a huge step towards being more selfless. In order to implement a universal basic income we must Love each other and respect each other as equals.

CHAPTER 20:
WORLD PEACE

I s world peace really possible in the 21st century?

World peace is a controversial topic. We learn about it as children and hold out hope it's possible. Once we get older we become more jaded and start believing that the world just, "works this way."

World peace seems like a pipe dream to the normal person. Definitely things are only seen to be getting worse as every passing day goes by. It seems at this rate that we will never attain world peace.

It seems unlikely now but it's entirely in the realm of possibility. Since 1945 we have seen fewer and fewer wars between countries and the number of deaths from warfare has been dropping.

Think about these sobering statistics: in 1958, only 4% of Americans approved of interracial marriage. 87% of Americans approve of it today. That's a drastic change over the course of one lifetime. It's hard for us to realize this now but for most of human history Europeans were at war with other Europeans. People in France saw people in Germany as subhuman and vice versa. These views are rarely ever held today.

Imagine traveling back in time to the year 1800 and convincing a group of men that all women should have the right to vote. Remember that women can not vote, can not own property and a man can legally abuse his wife. How would you go about convincing these men? It has become so normalized for us in today's world but to them the concept would have seemed obscure and alien. Now, women have the right to vote in over a hundred countries across the world.

Imagine telling a slave trader in the year 1700 that slavery is wrong. In that time, you could murder a slave and receive no punishment. Today, and extremely few people believe that slavery is right.

We still do things like this today. We're okay with eating poultry, pork, and beef but we're against the eating of dogs and cats. In the future, they will look back on what we do today and be mortified at what we did. Things that we don't even consider or know today will be commonplace in the future.

I say all this to point towards the fact that we don't know what's possible for our future. Things that seem out of reach now are entirely possible but only if we have an open mind. In our lifetimes we could implement a world government with one shared military. You may not think it's possible now but history shows that we're moving in that direction.

Why Self-Love? A world government with world peace would be the deepest form of Self-Love. It would truly show that we Love each other and value each other as equals. World peace is not possible if we carry hate in our hearts but it is entirely possible if we care enough about the world around us.

EPILOGUE

I f you've found value from this book, be sure to keep it as your essential guide for living a fulfilled life. Whenever you encounter a problem you don't know how to overcome, be sure to come back to this book and find the advice you need to overcome resistance.

If there's one thing I want you to take away from this book it's that Self-Love is a more powerful concept than most people imagine. Nearly all problems can be solved with Self-Love. With Self-Love you have the potential to let go of the weights holding you down and reach your highest human potential.

I've thoroughly enjoyed writing this book and I'm glad you could gain something from it. If there's any advice or criticism you would like to give me, feel free to reach out to me at neilvisvanathan@gmail.com.

Be sure to check out my blog where I upload new content almost every day. You can find the blog at developedmind.org or on YouTube as DevelopedMind.

I would like to thank you again for giving this book a read and I hope it was able to shine a light on how you can utilize Self-Love to improve your life.

Why Self-Love? Because you deserve it.

REFERENCES

Bregman, Rutger, et al. *Utopia for Realists: the Case for a Universal Basic Income, Open Borders, and a 15-Hour Workweek.* The Correspondent, 2016.

Yang, Andrew. *The War on Normal People The Truth About America's Disappearing Jobs and Why Universal Basic Income Is Our Future.* Hachette Books, 2019.